New Orleans Homes
at Christmas

TO: Jack and Rachel
Best holiday Wishes
Bonnie Warren

New Orleans Homes at Christmas

Bonnie Warren

Photography by
Cheryl Gerber

Foreword by Peggy Scott Laborde

PELICAN PUBLISHING COMPANY
GRETNA 2014

*The word "Pelican" and the depiction of a pelican are
trademarks of Pelican Publishing Company, Inc., and are
registered in the U.S. Patent and Trademark Office.*

Library of Congress Cataloging-in-Publication Data

Warren, Bonnie (Freelance writer)
  New Orleans homes at Christmas / by Bonnie Warren ; photography by Cheryl Gerber ;
foreword by Peggy Scott Laborde.
    pages cm
   ISBN 978-1-4556-1985-6 (hardcover : alk. paper) — ISBN 978-1-4556-1986-3 (e-book) 1.
Christmas decorations. 2.   Historic buildings—Louisiana—New Orleans. 3.   Dwellings—
Louisiana—New Orleans. I. Title.
  TT900.C4W376 2014
  745.594'120976335—dc23
                                                                        2014020731

Printed in China
Published by Pelican Publishing Company, Inc.
1000 Burmaster Street, Gretna, Louisiana 70053

To Evan Crone, my grandson, who is a constant source of joy, and to Rev. John Willis and Della West Warren, my wonderful parents, who spent sixteen years as missionaries in South Africa, where I was born, for teaching me the true meaning of Christmas

—Bonnie Warren

To my mother, Andre Gerber, who always filled our home with Christmas magic

—Cheryl Gerber

CONTENTS

FOREWORD

If ever there is a holiday where decorating is so much a part of a celebration, it's Christmas.

In New Orleans's early days, most of the residents' time was spent in surviving and, ultimately, constructing cottages that faced two fires and numerous hurricanes. By the 1830s, more time was available for decorating the substantial French Quarter townhouses born out of the success of commerce, thanks to the city's crucial port location along the Mississippi River.

For the holidays, indigenous plants decorated mantels. Tiny candles were affixed to wax myrtles, with a water bucket always stationed nearby. On display would be cardboard cutouts of the Nativity, printed in Europe. Before the locally grown fruit, such as lemons and oranges, became ingredients in the holiday meal, it would often be artfully arranged on the dining room table.

Fast-forwarding a century, New Orleans florists relished in their holiday greenery. Farley's, one of the city's most beloved plant purveyors, even served as a Christmas-season destination, since its greenhouses were brimming with decorations and greenery to behold.

From the mid-nineteenth century up to the 1980s, residents could purchase Christmas decorations on Canal Street from myriad department stores. Store windows certainly evoked the season, and the streetlamps on the neutral ground, or street median, resembled candy canes one year and became wreath bearers the next. For almost forty years, the City of New Orleans even had an official decorator, Betty Finnin, who made sure the historic cast-iron lamp poles were festooned for both the Christmas and Carnival seasons.

John Magill, senior curator/historian for The Historic New Orleans Collection, and I penned the book *Christmas in New Orleans* for Pelican Publishing in 2009. We showcased some homes that were famous for their exterior Christmas decorations. The lavishly decorated Centanni family home on Canal Street in the Mid-City neighborhood even featured a "Santa's Workshop," complete with mechanized elves "sawing." A life-size Santa figure could be seen stationed at the top of one of the home's chimneys.

For more than thirty-five years, Popeyes Chicken and Biscuits founder Al Copeland presented wonderlands with themes that included outer space. His enormous lighted figures of reindeer and snowmen is the stuff of fond local Christmas memories.

But enough of the past! In *New Orleans Homes at Christmas,* Bonnie Warren and Cheryl Gerber allow us a peek inside the homes of some notable locals. Bonnie, who is the home and garden editor of *New Orleans Magazine,* where she is a monthly contributor, has featured hundreds of homes in her column since the 1980s, as well as having contributed to national magazines such as *Better Homes and Gardens* since the late 1960s. Her knack for choosing residences has provided readers with a wealth of useful advice.

In *New Orleans Homes at Christmas,* New Orleans archbishop Gregory

Aymond's home, along with that of New Orleans Saints football team owners Tom and Gayle Benson commemorate the season in a more traditional yet elegant way. Archbishop Aymond's table-top statue of the Madonna and Christ Child with an Advent wreath placed directly in front of it is a poignant visual reminder of the reason for the season. The Bensons' display of glass and metal ornaments sparkles on a small metal stand. Bells, portraits of the Madonna, and crosses hanging are precious holiday reminders.

Using local greenery such as branches brimming with kumquats along with magnolia leaves to decorate the front door of his home, Hal Williamson also pays homage to the city's past in a graceful and traditional way.

We have grown to love and savor the historic homes that are open to the public in Christmas dress. Both the nineteenth-century Hermann-Grima House and Gallier House give us a rare view of the way antebellum New Orleanians commemorated the holiday. Longue Vue House and Gardens, along with the Williams Residence, show us the twentieth century, but with a respect for the past.

Another treat in this book are more contemporary approaches to holiday decorating. Chet Pourciau's stark white wooden Christmas tree cut-out is punctuated with tiny brackets just the right size for votive candle holders. Against a backdrop of compelling contemporary art, Jim Mounger and Eric Hess's ode to snowflakes is both beautiful and playful (snow being a rarity, thanks to our sub-tropical climate).

Since the 1970s, the Preservation Resource Center has presented a home tour featuring some of the historic Garden District's most lavishly decorated mansions. Bonnie and Cheryl have included seven homes whose owners have kindly their opened their private spaces for viewing on behalf of the center's primary fundraiser.

Also "under the tree" in this book are recipes of réveillon dinners from some of the city's finest restaurants. This culinary tradition, once again stemming from our French roots, consists of a multi-course meal served usually after midnight mass at St. Louis Cathedral. The concept was revived by the French Quarter Festival and embraced by local restaurants more than thirty years ago. Its popularity has skyrocketed.

Thanks to Bonnie and Cheryl, readers will have a chance to see how some creative New Orleanians deck their halls. *New Orleans Homes at Christmas* captures the spirit of the city today with its reverence for its rich past.

Peggy Scott Laborde, author of Christmas in New Orleans
and senior producer and host for WYES-TV

New Orleans Homes at Christmas

ARCHBISHOP GREGORY AYMOND

Christmas Style

Enter the home of Archbishop Gregory Aymond

on the campus of the Notre Dame Seminary on South Carrollton Avenue, and you will experience a special, sacred feeling. Reminders of the birth of Jesus, the origin in the celebration of Christmas, are everywhere, from portraits of the Blessed Virgin Mary and baby Jesus to statues gracing the vestibule and the reception room walls and nearby tables. Inside the vestibule, a handsome winding stairway, lined with festive red poinsettias, will lead you to the sacred chapel that truly makes this home unique.

The home was designed by architect Allison Owen and built by contractor Joseph Fromherz in 1926, with the chapel added during the 1935 renovations under the direction of Archbishop Joseph Rummel. The chapel is a unique space with an elaborate ceiling that presents the motif of the *Te Deum,* which is sung every year on January 8 to fulfill the promise made by then-Bishop-elect Louis-Guillaume-Valentin Dubourg and the Ursuline nuns after the victory in the Battle of New Orleans.

The stained glass windows in the chapel represent the patrons of the Archdiocese of New Orleans: the Blessed Virgin Mary; St. Joseph; St. Louis, King of France; and St. Vincent de Paul. "The reason Vincent de Paul became a secondary patron was because the first conference of the Society of St. Vincent de Paul in the United States was established in New Orleans," explains Emilie Gagnet Leumas, archivist for the Archdiocese of New Orleans.

"The chapel is my place of peace and refuge," explains Archbishop Aymond, the fourteenth archbishop of New Orleans and the first New Orleans native to serve in that capacity in the 216-year history of the local church. "I use it daily. It is a special place for me to meet our loving God, to reflect on the life of Christ, and on my own life. I pray daily for the people of the

OPPOSITE: The elaborate ceiling presents the motif of the *Te Deum,* which is sung every year on January 8 to fulfill the promise made by then-Bishop-elect Louis-Guillaume-Valentin Dubourg and the Ursuline nuns after the victory in the Battle of New Orleans.

BELOW: Built in 1926, the home of the Archbishop of the New Orleans Diocese is located on the grounds of the Notre Dame Seminary.

Archdiocese, the needs of the local Church, and all of the ministries that serve our local community."

The home has always been used as the residence of the archbishop of New Orleans since it was built. In September 1987, Pope John Paul II resided in the Archbishop's residence during his visit to New Orleans, and it is easy to understand why Archbishop Aymond named the residence in honor of him.

Gayle Benson (Mrs. Tom Benson) is credited with the renovation of the first

TOP LEFT: The parlor is furnished comfortably. Interior designer Gayle Benson reappointed and updated the house to capture the original beauty and history of a building that dates back almost ninety years.

TOP RIGHT: A Christmas tree rests on a table in front of a window in the vestibule.

BOTTOM LEFT: Historic Bibles have a place of honor on the coffee table in the parlor.

OPPOSITE: The Blessed Mother and baby Jesus are the subjects of both the portrait and statue in the vestibule.

floor, which includes the vestibule flanked by a parlor, reception, and dining rooms. "Gayle generously reappointed and updated the house to capture the original beauty and history of a building that dates back almost ninety years," Archbishop Aymond says.

Christmas is a special time in the Archbishop's residence. "Throughout the Christmas season, I have gatherings at the house with people who serve in ministry for the Archdiocese, and we also have special holiday meals in the dining room from time to time."

ABOVE: The winding stairway was added in the 1935 renovation to provide access to the second-floor chapel.

LEFT: A statue of Santa Claus respectfully pays homage to baby Jesus.

Archbishop Aymond is ever respectful that the house is very much a part of the history of the Archdiocese of New Orleans. "I enjoy the opportunity to use my residence as a place to meet with people from around the Archdiocese," he says.

ABOVE: Furnished in fine antiques, the dining room is the setting for special dinners.

LEFT: St. Louis Cathedral is replicated in one of the chapel's stained glass windows.

BRYAN BATT AND TOM CIANFICHI

Christmas Style

What would you expect of the home of an award-

OPPOSITE: The dining room is a study in elegance. Illuminated with an antique crystal chandelier, the table is dressed in fine china that once belong to Bryan's mother, sterling flatware from his grandmother, and linen napkins from Hazelnut. Mario Villa designed the chairs.

BELOW: The two-story home, on a quiet Uptown street, features the living and dining rooms on the second floor to take advantage of the balcony.

winning Broadway, television, and film actor, not to mention the author of two books and owner of premiere gift shops in New Orleans and Mandeville? Find out in the home of Bryan Batt, whose star-studded list of credits includes nine Broadway shows as well as the multi-award-winning *Mad Men* television series. It is here, on a quiet street in an Uptown neighborhood, where he resides with his partner, Tom Cianfichi, who manages and co-owns Hazelnut, their much-touted gift shops.

"We both adore Christmas, and we decorate our home with a masculine elegance with a definite sprinkling of whimsy," Bryan says. The living and dining rooms both have a glamorous Hollywood Regency vibe reminiscent of a 1930s movie set, but the kitchen lounging area is all about relaxation and comfort. That is where their dogs—Peggy, a Boston Terrier, and Pip, a rescue Yorkie—romp and play while the gentlemen sip coffee or spiked eggnog from nostalgic heirloom Christmas china.

"Today, everything is a tad toned down from our elaborate Christmas decorations in our one-bedroom Manhattan co-op, where we would relocate some of the furniture into the hallway, wire the loaded Christmas tree to the wall, and host what came to be 'the' holiday party of the Broadway set. It would be wall-to-wall full of people, very much like a Holly Golightly fête, with Tom, the great cook in our home, preparing gumbo and turtle soup for our guests. Now, with two Hazelnut locations, we are so busy during the holidays that we are lucky if we even remember to bring out my mom's Christmas china."

The couple still finds time to install a floor-to-ceiling blue spruce tree and load it with beloved ornaments collected over a lifetime together. "Tom and I do all the decorating," Bryan says. "Tom is so talented with visuals—and having a fine gift and home accents shop doesn't hurt."

Bryan, who adds designer to his list of job titles, is quick to share some of his Christmas-decorating mantras. "You can never have too many lights or ornaments on a tree. The lights should be woven in and out of the branches, from the tiptop of the tree all the way down to the trunk.

Colorful balls can be placed deep within the branches to add depth of color and layering." Then he smiles and adds, "Go for the wow factor. Colorful new ornaments hanging next to those from both of my grandmothers always make me smile."

Bryan also has author credits to his name. While his second book is all about design and New Orleans homes, his first book (a "momoir," as he terms it) pays tribute to his late mother, Gayle Batt, whom he credits with helping to cultivate his unique sense of style. "I grew up with wonderful Christmas memories," he says. "When I was a boy, my mother and I shared the love of decorating for every holiday imaginable, but Christmas was our favorite. We had Christmas trees and decorations all over the house, even our bedrooms. I love the fact that until her dying day, she decorated with the same fervor for her granddaughters as she did in my youth. Yes, you could say I inherited my mother's decorating gene. I don't even know what the words 'over the top' mean."

Today, the house represents Bryan's inheritance of his mother's enthusiasm for holiday decorating with his own somewhat funky, modern eye, combined with his love of elegance, as evidenced in the dining room, to create a joyful, eclectic Christmas showplace.

TOP LEFT: A silver-painted garland and pine cones are used on the stairway.

TOP RIGHT: A colorful Christopher Radko masked merrymaker.

BOTTOM RIGHT: A John Clemmer painting hangs over the antique Biedermeier chest, flanked by a pair of Louis XV chairs. The statue of a stylized head topped with a Christmas hat has a place of honor on the marble top.

OPPOSITE: Sweets are served in the lounge area of the kitchen.

GAYLE AND TOM BENSON

Christmas Style

Located on a private street just off St. Charles Avenue, the stately home of Gayle and Tom Benson is immediately set apart from the other grand houses on the broad boulevard by its black canvas drapes, embossed at the top with a gold *fleur-de-lis,* which hang over the entrance to the front porch. If the hangings didn't give it away, stepping inside will immediately reveal the connection between the homeowners and the National Football League's New Orleans Saints team. Tom is the proud owner of the New Orleans Saints (and the National Basketball Association's New Orleans Pelicans), and, as you may suspect, the home has a large collection of Saints memorabilia, including many items the couple collected from the Saints' prize-winning Super Bowl XLIV game in 2010.

Gayle, a talented interior designer, hasn't let the sports treasures get in the way of creating an elegant home that does double duty, being used to entertain a large group of casually dressed guests or a few select visitors decked out in their finest for an elegant sit-down dinner at a table with appointments fit for a king and queen.

"We especially enjoy our home during the Christmas season, when our goal is to always keep true to the meaning of the season," she says. "The Nativity scene in our front yard welcomes you in the true spirit of Christmas." Both Gayle and Tom are devout Catholics.

The formal area of the home includes the parlor, library, and dining room, with a broad foyer in the center of the floor plan. Leaded glass double doors, topped by a matching transom, add warm natural light

RIGHT: Gayle and Tom Benson live in a stately home on a gated street just off St. Charles Avenue.

to the space, while the windows in the parlor are dressed in fine silk and softly draped, giving a warm glow to the room. It is here in the parlor that the eye takes in the unique Christmas-related treasures, such as a gold-leaf display stand on top of an antique round table filled with sentimental sterling silver ornaments collected over the years. Another antique round table rests on the other side of the damask-covered sofa and features an eclectic collection that includes a Royal Dalton statue of a pregnant

ABOVE: Furnished in fine antiques with drapes of heavy silk covering the windows, the parlor is a study in elegance. A portrait of Gayle by Garland Robinette hangs over the marble fireplace.

LEFT: A large Nativity scene has a place of honor in the front yard.

23

Blessed Mother Mary, a gift from Archbishop Gregory Aymond. Many of the decorations have special meaning because they are gifts from friends. "I believe good design should always incorporate things with special sentimental meaning, side by side with fine furnishings and accessories," Gayle says.

Of special interest in the parlor is the large portrait of Gayle by Garland Robinette, their good friend, artist, and radio-show host, which has a place of honor over the marble fireplace.

The picture-perfect dining room comfortably seats sixteen guests at the broad, antique table. Gayle had the walls and ceiling given a special bronze finish to add to the feeling of elegance. Here, like in every room on the first level of the Benson's home, there is a Christmas tree. "We create an individual Christmas tree for [each of our] five great grandchildren and two great nieces, and all of the gifts under that tree are for one person," she says.

Once you step into the cozy back rooms of the house, your eyes will feast on the sports-laden memorabilia of all descriptions. "This is where we both share the ups and downs of the Saints and Pelicans. Most of all, our home is a place of refuge and comfort and to enjoy special times such as the Christmas season."

OPPOSITE, TOP LEFT: A framed poster honoring the Saints as the champions of Super Bowl XLIV rests on the floor next to a decorated umbrella, while a bound volume commemorating the victory sits on the large antique desk.

OPPPOSITE, TOP RIGHT: A portrait of Tom hangs over the fireplace. The Christmas angel shares the table with a painting of the Saints' *fleur-de-lis*.

OPPPOSITE, BOTTOM LEFT: The grand dining room features a broad table that seats sixteen.

OPPPOSITE, BOTTOM RIGHT: A gold charger holds the fine china plate and Christmas napkin, wrapped in a sterling silver napkin ring.

RIGHT: A unique tree-shaped gold-leaf stand atop a damask-covered antique table displays the couple's collection of sterling silver Christmas ornaments.

NANCY
CALHOUN

Christmas Style

Each Christmas season, a

statue of a pelican adorned with a big red bow greets visitors near the front door of the English Turn home of Nancy Calhoun. Above, massive Corinthian columns with banisters on the broad balcony are draped with holiday greenery attached by red bows. Even the unique widow's walk surrounding the rooftop copula is decked with garlands and bows. Here is a home where Christmas is celebrated to its fullest.

Built in the Greek Revival style of great plantation mansions, the unique home was completed twenty years ago by Nancy and her late husband, Dr. Milburn Calhoun. Hugging the banks of a lazy lagoon with a vast pastoral view of the green space beyond, the home is a showplace designed by architect George D. Hopkins Jr.

"A great deal of planning and thought went in to everything in our home, from the selection of the lot to the exterior and interior design," explains Nancy, who is still active in Pelican Publishing Company, one of the premiere mid-sized publishing operations in the country, which was guided to its current success by her husband, who was also a practicing physician.

"Christmas is the time of the year when I look forward to the tall tree going up in the living room and house being dressed in all its holiday glory," Nancy says with a smile. "We love to share Christmas with family and friends, and we planned our home to make sure we had plenty of room to enjoy holiday entertaining.

"It is a happy time when the Christmas ritual of decorating

ABOVE: The clear view of the nearby lagoon and green space beyond is evident through the French doors that open onto the rear veranda.

TOP RIGHT: Designed by architect George D. Hopkins Jr., the Greek Revival-style home in English Turn features Corinthian columns and a cupola surrounded by a widow's walk.

BOTTOM: A stately pelican graced with a red bow provides a welcome near the front door.

the tree with ornaments of special sentimental importance occurs. The top of the tree still has the same lighted star that once belonged to my mother, and I cherish the original box that has a price tag of twenty-five cents attached to the top."

Nancy's four granddaughters, Susan, Leslie, Sophia, and Heather Calhoun, have contributed meaningful ornaments to the tree, as has Sharon, her daughter-in-law, and David, her son, a professor of philosophy at Gonzaga University in Spokane, Washington. Kathleen Nettleton, Nancy's daughter and president of Pelican Publishing Company, and Carl, Kathleen's husband, also have contributed their share of ornaments over the years. "I just smile when Lori Ryan Solano [of Fancy Flowers], who has done the decorating of the house for Christmas for years, suggests a theme for our tree," Nancy says. "'No, Lori, we never do themes'—we fondly do memories for our tree."

OPPOSITE, TOP LEFT: The open floor plan offers a dramatic view of the downstairs from the foyer to the two stories of fan windows. French doors provide access to the veranda and backyard.

OPPOSITE, TOP RIGHT: Poinsettias decorate the antique table in the foyer, and red bows adorn the sconces on either side of the mirror.

OPPOSITE, BOTTOM: The curved balcony, decorated with garland and red bows, showcases the two-story living room with its tall Christmas tree. The balcony provides access to the wings on either side of the second floor.

ABOVE: The rear of the home takes full advantage of the lagoon and picturesque green space through the large windows.

RIGHT: A cherished wooden pelican is part of the sentimental collection of ornaments, dating from when Nancy was a child. Each one has a special meaning to the family.

The festive holiday home especially comes to life when family and friends gather after the Christmas Eve service at church to open their presents under the tree. Happy voices join in the singing of traditional Christmas carols, and a grand meal completes the evening. "On Christmas morning, we explore the contents of our individual stockings that hang from the circular stairway. There is always a special excitement to see what each stocking holds," Nancy continues. "Every corner of the living room is filled with happy voices and laughter, and while the dining room may be center stage for meals, even Milburn's large desk in the library does double duty as a dining table, along with the breakfast room table, and even card tables are sometimes called in to service."

Christmas highlights the uniqueness of the house in the library, Milburn's favorite space and the *pièce de résistance*, dressed with garlands and red bows. The two-story space just inside the front door is complete with a winding staircase fashioned after the one in the movie *My Fair Lady* and a 1780 fifteen-foot wide mahogany breakfront/bookcase that was purchased long before the home was built and carefully stored, just waiting for its perfect home. The floor-to-ceiling bookcases on both levels house the couple's library, which numbers thousands of books and gets a special Christmas face to match the garlands and bows of the other rooms.

"There is much I enjoy about our home, but my favorite feature is the open floor plan that provides an unobstructed

OPPOSITE: The winding staircase in the library was inspired by the one in the movie *My Fair Lady.*

ABOVE: The two-level library was built to accommodate the couple's extensive collection of books.

view from the front door, past the winding staircase," Nancy says. "The view embraces the main living space with its twenty-foot-high ceiling and two levels of arched windows that overlook the veranda and the beautiful view of the lagoon and green space beyond." She quickly adds, "This is a home that was meant to be shared with family and friends. It seems to especially welcome and embrace you at Christmastime. To me, just stepping inside the home says 'Welcome—come inside and enjoy Christmas.'"

OPPOSITE: The dining room table is covered in a festive green tablecloth in keeping with the holiday season.

ABOVE: A bay window in the master bedroom provides a panoramic view of the lagoon and green landscape. A pair of comfortable chairs offers a tranquil spot for reading and relaxing.

RIGHT: A fireplace adds to the coziness of the den during the holiday season.

SUE ELLEN AND
JOSEPH "JOE" CANIZARO

Christmas Style

The Christmas season is

a special time for Sue Ellen and Joseph "Joe" Canizaro. Their Metairie Club Gardens home takes on a special glow with festive decorations, but it is in their sacred chapel that the true spirit of Christmas is celebrated in a special way: paying homage to the birth of Jesus with a solemn mass shared with family and friends. "When we built our new home, one of our first requests to our architect was to design a chapel," Joe explains. "We wanted it to be at the core of our home in a sunny spot overlooking the fountain and garden."

While the Canizaros' home is an architectural and interior-design gem that was featured on several pages of *Architectural Digest* magazine and on the cover of *The Language of Interior Design* by Alexa Hampton, their internationally acclaimed interior designer, it is also a warm and inviting home often shared with non-profit groups such as Longue Vue House and Gardens for a fundraising event and religious groups associated with their Catholic faith.

First-time visitors may marvel at the grandeur of the antiques and accessories, yet it is the Canizaros' collection of religious art that takes center stage in the home. "I began collecting in 1993, and today we have about fifty cataloged religious works of art," Joe explains as he conducts a personal tour of each room, describing in great detail the title, history of the piece, and information about each artist. "Someday I hope all of the paintings will be part of a religious art gallery for the public to enjoy."

Designed by New Orleans architect Peter M. Trapolin and built by Michael A. LaForte Jr. of Vintage Construction Company of New Orleans, Inc., the house took four years to construct. "Peter did an outstanding job designing our home, Michael was a great contractor,

ABOVE: A treasured painting from circa 1480, *Adoration of Christ,* by the famous Italian artist Sandro Botticelli, has a place of honor over the fireplace in the library.

TOP RIGHT: Designed by architect Peter A. Trapolin and built by Michael LaForte Jr., the Canizaros' home is a showcase that has been featured in *Architectural Digest* magazine and on the cover of *The Language of Interior Design,* a book written by their interior designer, Alexa Hampton.

and we can't say enough good things about Alexa, who gave us everything we wanted in a formal yet comfortable home," says Joe, the founder, chairman, and CEO of Columbus Properties LP, a commercial real estate development company; the president of First Trust Corporation, which includes the First Bank and Trust; and a well-known philanthropist.

"We are pleased that so many of the antiques and accessories in our home came from the great antique shops in New Orleans," Sue Ellen says, and she also notes that it was local artisans who did the first-class job on the details throughout the house.

"This was an ideal home for us," she adds when asked how she feels about their showplace residence that graces a tree-lined boulevard in one of the finest

ABOVE: The sun-filled living room is furnished with fine antiques and accessories, many of which were selected from New Orleans antique shops. Internationally acclaimed Alexa Hampton is credited with the interior design.

LEFT: Cherished Christmas decorations collected over the years adorn the tree in the family room.

OPPOSITE: The grand staircase in the rotunda is further dramatized by the marble floor and majestic antique crystal chandelier.

neighborhoods in the New Orleans area. "It is always a pleasure to share our home with family and friends. The dining room is one of my favorite spaces, and it is a joy to entertain with intimate lunches and dinners." Joe is quick to add that he also enjoys their home. "It always feels good to come home to such pleasant surroundings, and I am ever humble in appreciation for the blessing of having such a comfortable home."

Sue Ellen and Joe concur that the Christmas season is their favorite time of year to enjoy their home. "We especially love the chapel, with its handcrafted pews and altar created by Thomas Bruno, New Orleans sculptor and furniture maker, and the sacred art treasures make it even

OPPOSITE: The dramatic dining room is a study in grandeur, with columns framing the glass French doors that overlook the pool and side garden. Interior designer Alexa Hampton designed the table and chairs, making the latter larger and more comfortable than usual antique chairs.

TOP LEFT: The 1602 oil on copper painting by Guido Reni is entitled *Holy Family with St. John the Baptist*.

TOP RIGHT: Sue Ellen's favorite painting is *Young Girl with Bowl* by William-Adolphe Bouguereau.

BOTTOM: The table setting is in keeping with the grandeur of the dining room.

more special at Christmastime," he says.

Both agree that the entire mood of the home changes once the holiday decorations are in place. The architecture, interior design, and noted art collection simply become an interesting backdrop for a house that is filled with unique and colorful Christmas adornment.

LEFT: A circa-1790 terra cotta statue of a Louis XVI-style woman has a place of honor in the rotunda.

ABOVE: Thomas Bruno, New Orleans sculptor and furniture maker, made the altar and benches for the chapel. A mosaic of the young holy family was created by a young artist at the Vatican's mosaic shop, while other religious works of art include *(top right)* a fifteenth-century painting of the crucifixion and death of Jesus and *(bottom right)* Christ Carrying the Cross, by Andrea Solario.

RIGHT: The broad loggia allows light to flood the house through a series of arched windows and French doors.

ERIC HESS AND FRANK THAXTON

Christmas Style

It's Christmas on Bayou St. John, and nothing

OPPOSITE: Roland Montealegre of Urban Earth made the unique Christmas "tree" from white-painted branches. It is decorated with glass ornaments made by artist Mitchell Gaudet.

BELOW: Chocolate chip cookies are served on a tray decorated with blue ornaments.

is decked out in red and green. Instead, the landmark contemporary home on Moss Street takes on a modern twenty-first-century splendor of white twig "trees," decked out in hand-blown blue and gold ornaments, gifts wrapped in colorful wallpaper and tied with large bows, and a dining room table dressed in Lomonosov porcelain from St. Petersburg, Russia, straight from the opulent era of Russian Czars.

This isn't your ordinary Christmas home. The beauty of the home of Eric Hess, president/CEO of Hess Marketing, and Frank Thaxton, a retired Shreveport judge, is sleek and grand as well as unusual and treasure-filled. There are cupcakes topped with blue, white, and chocolate icing placed carefully on an antique silver tray filled with tiny blue gel balls, chocolate-chip cookies surrounded with blue Christmas baubles of various sizes, and a dining room table adorned with a twig centerpiece draped with tiny blue vases filled with white flowers.

"Because our home is contemporary, our holiday decorations are in keeping with the style of the architecture and interior design," Eric explains. "We definitely break away from the traditional Christmas tree, but at the same time, we keep the idea of a tree alive with the unique branch interpretation that Roland Montealegre of Urban Earth created. He sprayed the branches white, then added tiny blue lights to incorporate the basic color we used as our holiday theme.

"We used blue lights to dress the branches of the trees that display hand-blown blue ornaments from artist Mitchell Gaudet. We collect Mitchell's work, and while we did add other ornaments to the tree and on the twig centerpiece on the dining room table, it's Mitchell's hand-blown Christmas ornaments that help to make the decorations unique."

Montealegre also developed the centerpiece for the dining room table. "We knew he would do something a bit over the top and unique," Eric says. "We placed blue gel balls in the champagne glasses

43

to bring the eye to the centerpiece and then added a gift for each guest atop the place settings. Blue wired ribbon added that special final touch to the wrapped gifts."

"Celebrating Christmas for us means being with family," Frank explains. "We trade off each year and switch celebrating Thanksgiving and Christmas at our homes in either New Orleans or Shreveport. The season involves dinners at home with friends and family and a seasonal party. Food is a big part of Christmas, and especially sweets, so creating unique cakes and desserts are a part of the way we celebrate."

Christmas on Bayou St. John may not be red and green, but it couldn't be more festive at the home of Eric and Frank.

OPPOSITE, TOP: The home, featuring a large living room with a corner window wall and French doors, overlooks Bayou St. John. Eric painted the art above the tables to the left, John Palmer's art is on the right wall, and glass blower Mitchell Gaudet's work sits underneath.

OPPOSITE, BOTTOM: French doors open to provide an unobstructed view of Bayou St. John.

RIGHT: Hand-blown Christmas ornaments decorate the branches fashioned into a modern Christmas tree.

BELOW: Individual gifts are placed on top of each place setting, Lomonosov porcelain resting on a gold charger. Blue gel balls in champagne glasses add interest to the table, which has a centerpiece fashioned of twigs.

WILLIAM "BILLY" LEYSATH AND ARCHIE SAURAGE

Christmas Style

Begin with a historic showplace

on Esplanade Avenue, and then dress it up with breathtaking holiday decorations—you will have a magic winter wonderland. Located in the Faubourg St. John neighborhood near City Park, homeowner William "Billy" Leysath enlists the help of Archie Saurage each year to compose the elaborate decorations of both the inside and outside of the unique home.

"Christmas is a special time of the year," Billy explains. "The house just lends itself to dressing up for the holidays. We drape garland across the front iron fence and gate and fill the large pots on the balcony with live poinsettias. Garland is also added around the tall pair of front doors."

The outside decorations definitely make the house an attraction for lovers of elaborately decorated holiday homes, but here, everything is done very tastefully and without lighted angels or animated Santa Claus figures. "Even the tour busses slow down when they pass the house," Billy adds.

Built in 1902 by William J. Hannon, an Irishman, master carpenter, and real estate speculator who owned a lumber mill in St. Tammany Parish, the mansion features some of the finest millwork in the city. The Queen Anne-style residence has a turret with multi-colored slate shingles and fancy jigsaw work. The exterior contains the usual filigree of Victorian houses, such as gingerbread millwork and spindles. It features a wrap-around porch and an impressive pair of winding stairways leading from the ground level to the main floor. The 12-by-86-foot center hall occupies more

RIGHT: Called the "Crown Jewel of Esplanade Avenue," the Queen Anne-style mansion was built in 1902.

than 1,000 square feet, reportedly the longest hallway in a private residence in New Orleans—not including the 4-by-12-foot foyer.

"I especially like the fact that the integrity of the house has never been compromised," Billy says about his home. "It still has three sets of double pocket doors fitted between the 12-inch double-thick walls, and single pocket doors in the rest of the house. All of the chandeliers are original to the house, and the nine fireplaces and mantels remain as when they were built."

ABOVE: Adjoining parlors all feature holiday decorations.

LEFT: Satsumas are frosted with sugar to give a holiday display a local flair.

"The center hall becomes a showcase for many of the dozen Christmas trees we feature each year," Archie explains. "Each one has a different theme, and nothing remains static from year to year; we are always adding new ornaments and decorations. Everything gets a touch of holiday decoration, with candles placed on the hallway hat rack and ribbons draped around the necks of the statues."

The triple parlors and adjoining dining room take on a special festival mode for the annual Christmas party Billy and Archie stage for friends and family. Billy usually plays the grand piano, and a feast is served from the long dining room table. "Sharing this house during the holiday season always brings me great joy," Billy says.

LEFT: A snowman ornament hangs among the tinsel in one of the Christmas trees.

ABOVE: The dining room is furnished with fine antiques.

Literature collected about the history of the mansion often calls it the "Crown Jewel of Esplanade Avenue," and it is easy to see why it was so honored. "There is so much to admire about this historic house," Billy adds. "Yes, it always pleases me to dress it up at Christmas for others to enjoy."

ABOVE: The 12-by-86-foot center hall provides plenty of space of space to display Christmas trees.

RIGHT: A carousel horse is decorated with plaid and gold ribbon.

JAMES A.
"JIM" MOUNGER

Christmas Style

Attorney James A. "Jim"

Mounger lives in an art gallery on a fashionable Uptown street just a few blocks from the Mississippi River. He has been a major patron of the arts in New Orleans for twenty-plus years, and his house is known for its museum-like display of contemporary art. If it's Christmastime and you pass Jim's impressive historic house, you would probably slow down and ask out loud, "Hey, what's going on with that house?" Windows, doors, balcony, and porch are painted the same neutral color, not to mention the seven huge urns dotting the porch and balcony that seem to have been colored from the same bucket. So, it may strike you as curious that the huge snowflake ornaments hanging from the ceiling of both porch and balcony are also the same color. The impact of the monochromatic color scheme probably makes people ask, "What's on the inside of that house?"

Well, the mostly open spaces of what was once a grand mansion are a visual feast. "I enjoy the drama of allowing the art to speak for itself, with everything else just a backdrop to enhance the visual pleasure of the art," Jim explains.

During the Christmas season, the house takes on a special glow with front-to-back-door holiday decorations, and you will find even more to see

TOP LEFT: Mylar garland and large snowflakes decorate the covered outdoor deck.

TOP RIGHT: The stately circa-1900 home is washed in the same color, from the porch and balcony floors to the doors and shutters.

on the back deck. "I always like dramatic and unusual decorations that Bently Graham delivers," Jim says.

"Jim and I have been collaborating for fifteen years on his holiday decorations," explains Bently, an event designer and display artist. "It is always an exciting project, since we never do the same thing twice and Jim is always open to something new and unique. We just pick a theme and go from there."

When Jim pitched the word "snowflakes," Bently replied, "Why, of course! What a perfect theme for such a magnificent house."

"The only thing I always know for sure each year is that nothing will be the usual cookie-cutter Christmas decorations," Jim adds.

Both agree that the usual green Christmas tree just won't cut it.

There is no mistake: this is not an ordinary house. Friends who visit during the holiday season never know what to expect. "They just know for sure that it won't be boring," Bently adds.

Purchased a dozen years ago, the circa-1900 house was a forlorn fourplex when Jim found it. He immediately enlisted the help of his friend John Chrestia, an architect and interior designer, to create maximum wall space to showcase his collection of paintings, sculpture, and other art objects.

Today, the showplace art gallery, contemporary

OPPOSITE: Nicole Charbonnet's painting *Batman* has a place of honor over the chest. The tall vases stuffed with white balls and snowflakes follow the theme of the holiday decorations. Snowflakes, white branches, and a tall crystal candlestick give a festive air to the room.

ABOVE: A large painting of Snow White fills the entire room, which also features a low glass table, sectional sofa, and two ottomans.

LEFT: A clear base vase holds a bouquet of snowflakes.

art museum, and home stands alone for uniqueness. These rooms can't have standard names such as living room, dining room, and den; rather, it's front gallery, center gallery, and rear gallery—but even so, it still feels like a livable space—a home.

One thing is certain: in December, Santa Claus never has a problem finding the monochrome structure with more art than fills some museums. "This is always a happy house," Jim says with a smile. "And I never tire of having Bently transform it into a holiday wonderland each year. I am already thinking of what a good theme would be for next year."

OPPOSITE: Snowflakes hang from the ceiling, and tall, cone-shaped objects allude to Christmas trees.

TOP LEFT: A Dale Chihuly glass sculpture in the middle of the front gallery becomes festive with the addition of snowflakes.

TOP RIGHT: The black towers with apple-shaped glass on top are by Neil Harshfield.

BOTTOM RIGHT: A pair of silver trees adds interest to the space, which also features a glass-topped wine rack.

JOHN WADE

Christmas Style

Hidden from the picturesque tree-

RIGHT: A corner Christmas tree has a place of honor in the living room, which is comfortably furnished with fine antiques. Interior designer Emily Adams designed the interiors and decorated them for the holiday season.

BELOW: A Christmas wreath hangs on the garland-framed front door, while a pair of live topiaries flanks each side. Outside decorations were created by Paula Gudaitis of Nature's Impressions.

lined street behind a brick fence, there isn't the slightest hint of John Wade's beautiful Garden District home. It's a secret treasure with a pristine formal garden separating the fence from the jewel of a mansion.

Bedecked in Christmas finery, the grandeur of the home is well fitted to be to be dressed for the holiday season. "John's home is a study of using fine antiques with contemporary accessories and warm colors to create rooms that are pleasing to the eye, yet comfortable," explains Emily Adams, the talented interior designer who created a livable space for him.

"I even found the house for him," she continues. "I had decorated his nearby condominium, and when he called me in to do some new things for the space, I simply said, 'Let's find you a nice house in the Garden District and not redo this place.'" John agreed, and soon she was hard at work making the new home she found something special.

"Emily knows my tastes," says John, an entrepreneur, an author, and the editor of *How to Achieve a Heaven on Earth,* a collection of 101 inspirational essays by local, national, and international leaders. "I immediately liked the private courtyard that adjoins the dining room, the formal gardens, and the large rear garden. The house gives me total privacy, and it's a quiet place to work."

John moved into the house in 2003. "It was a joy making the place his personal retreat," Emily offers. "I brought in decorative painter Bekye Fargason to work her magic with wall treatments

in the warm colors he loves. The soft gold and warm red-browns provided the perfect backdrop. I used shimmering antique gold, greens, and iridescent reds for the decorations instead of the usual bright red and green colors."

As for the holiday season, Emily wanted to use a more sophisticated theme for John. "He is a single gentleman with elegant taste, so I made sure not to include a Santa Claus or reindeers in my scheme of things. Instead, to reflect on the subject of his book, I used angels and *fleurs-de-lis*.

RIGHT: Red ribbon and a silver pinecone adorn John's books, which he gives to friends during the holiday season.

TOP LEFT: The focal point of the library is a large banner by Shreveport-New Orleans artist Lawrence Shor. A small Christmas tree has a place of honor on the small table in front of the banner.

TOP RIGHT: An antique bronze angel from Naghi's on Royal Street rests on a pedestal adorned with a red velvet bow. Bay leaves painted gold create the wreath on the wall.

BOTTOM LEFT: Pine branches and cones, along with red berries, a single red candle, and a small pine topiary grace the chest in the living room.

ABOVE: Sunlight from the garden
floods the dining room, where
champagne awaits guests.

OPPOSITE, BOTTOM RIGHT: A
painted Louis XVI chest serves
as the setting of the pair of
plaster angel candleholders,
while a pair of gilded lamps
flanks the angels. A wreath of
gold-painted bay leaves hangs
on the mirror above the chest.

He has a deep feeling for humanity, as well as New Orleans and his beloved Saints, so the *fleur-de-lis* was a perfect symbol for the major theme."

Instead of the usual large Christmas tree, Emily used three smaller trees of various shapes, sizes, and décor. Two large banners, each featuring stylized Byzantine angels, were painted by Shreveport-New Orleans artist Lawrence Shor. One banner is hung over the wall of bookcases in the library, and the other has a place of honor above the stairway landing.

"Emily did a great job decorating my home for the holidays," John says. "The joyful spirit of the holiday season lives all year in my home, and I can truthfully say this place has helped me to learn *How to Achieve a Heaven on Earth.*"

CAREY
HAMMETT

Designers' Holiday Magic

It's the holiday season in

Metairie Club Gardens, where grandeur still reins supreme. Step inside the home of interior designer Carey Hammett, and it is easy to imagine you are enjoying a bit of Paris for Christmas. "It's the time of year when you can enjoy French glamour," Carey explains, as she gives a tour of her chateau-style 1920s-era home decorated with exquisite French antiques. "Each room takes on a special glow during the holidays, and you can't have too many candles and bows to carry out the festive mood throughout the house."

The noted interior designer of some of the most interesting homes in the area always has been known for having an outstanding holiday home. Dual wreaths greet you at the front door, and when you step inside the vestibule, you will find white marble floors and twinkling, tiny white lights adorning the garland and gold bows dressing the winding stairway. "It is my way of welcoming family and friends to my home," she adds with a smile.

The French-influenced living room features red bows on the eighteenth-century antique chandelier, which is topped with angels. Garland and red bows decorate the marble fireplace, and candelabras flank the large, antique portrait of

TOP LEFT: Furnished in fine French antiques, the colorful, deep rose walls add glamour to the living room. An antique needlepoint rug is a handsome cover for the white and aubergine marble floors.

TOP RIGHT: Built in 1927 in the French chateau style, the Hammett home was one of the first completed in the Metairie Club Gardens area.

BOTTOM LEFT: A treasured silver reindeer and sleigh with gold overlay is used to display Christmas ornaments.

an elegantly dressed woman above the mantel. Floors are magnificent white and aubergine marble, adding to the chateau look of the room.

"I enjoy entertaining during the holiday season," the civic activist explains. "Dressing the dining room table with cherished silver, china, and crystal from my ancestors is a joy." The silk damask-covered walls and drapes in the dining room add to the festive mood, as does the gold leaf ceiling and molding. Here again the white and aubergine marble floors add glamour to the room.

"My Christmas decorations are special because they have been collected over the years and they are treasured by my children and grandchildren," Carey says. Of special interest is a group of ornaments that celebrate the Louisiana Governor's mansion. They were designed by Alice Foster, the wife of former governor Murphy J. 'Mike' Foster, and the Design Advisory Board, for the mansion. Carey served on the Design Advisory Board.

Tall, artificial Christmas trees are featured in the den and game room. "Everybody knows that I am a tree hugger," the noted preservationist adds. "I long ago stopped cutting down live trees for the house." She has been active in preserving the historic tree canopy in Metairie, with special emphasis on Metairie Club Gardens.

Created in 1926, Metairie Club Gardens is noted for open green spaces that were carved out of what was once a pastoral setting. "The beautiful double alley of oak trees on Northline Avenue is one of the great treasures of our neighborhood," she continues. "Metairie Club Gardens Association always decorates either end of the neutral ground with large wreaths to further enhance to festival holiday feeling in the area."

It is easy to understand why Carey's family and friends always look forward to visiting during the holiday season. Where else can you find a bit of Paris wrapped up so festively as in the stately home on a quiet street in Metairie?

Carey's husband, Donald, passed away a few years ago, but she pays homage to him in the warmth and welcome spirit of her home. "Donald loved Christmas when our children were young," she says as she pours tea from an antique silver teapot that once belonged to her grandmother. "He would be happy to know that the house is still filled with laughter and joy for the holiday season."

OPPOSITE, TOP: A large pot of poinsettias has a place of honor on the coffee table in the den, while the base of the palm tree, adorned with tiny lights, also is decorated with a large net ribbon.

OPPOSITE, BOTTOM: Large bows and garland illuminated with tiny white lights decorate the winding stairway.

ABOVE: A single angel above the elaborately dressed bed in the master bedroom is a subtle announcement that it's the holiday season.

RIGHT: A single red candle casts its light on the twinkling Christmas tree behind it.

CHET POURCIAU

Designers' Holiday Magic

Chet Pourciau's home seems

to sing with holiday joy. You know you are in for a treat as soon as you see the white canvas drapes over the double front doors of the pristine corner house in a quiet Carrollton neighborhood near St. Charles Avenue. While there is seldom snow for Christmas in New Orleans, it would be easy to say that the theme of this house is *I'm Dreaming of a White Christmas.*

A rising interior design star with his own show on WLAE-TV and many other national television appearances, Chet enjoys decorating with lots of white, a little silver, countless candles, and "out of the box" ideas. "Go for something different," he urges as he gives a tour of the exquisite home he shares with his partner, attorney Jack Sullivan.

Unique take-away ideas start with the Christmas tree constructed of plywood, which is adorned with more than fifty tiny ledges holding glowing votive battery-powered candles and a real candle at the very top,

"Ledges were added in a random manner to hold the candles, then the tree and ledges were covered with countless layers of wax," Chet says. "The best part is that you never have to worry about needles falling off of the limbs of this tree!" On the nearby coffee table, a small terrarium is filled with tiny lights and white and silver balls on a bed of artificial snow.

"You won't find ordinary Christmas stockings in this house," he says. "I found the wonderful stockings hanging on the wall at an AIDS benefit. They were created from white packing

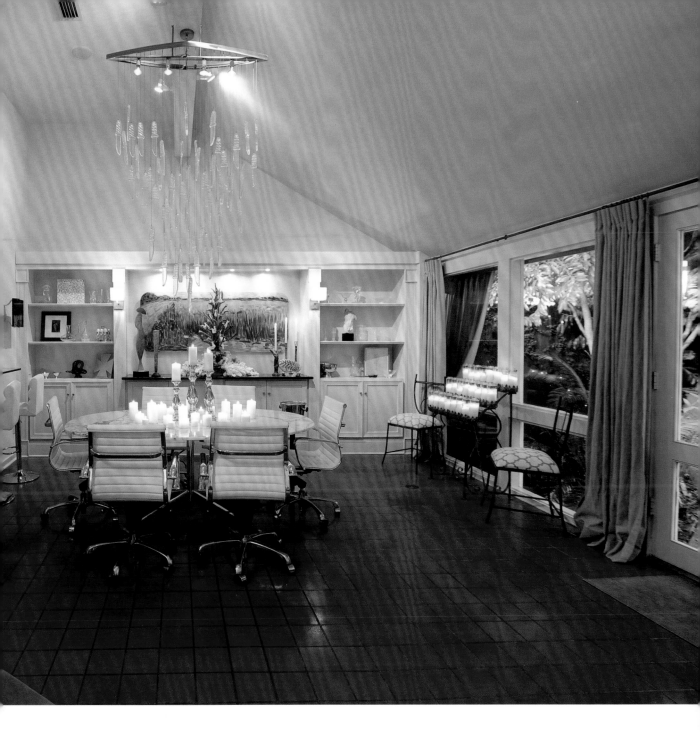

peanuts, adorned by snowflakes and tied with white ribbons." He inspects them closely, adding, "I think they make a terrific design statement."

OPPOSITE, LEFT: Built in 1895 as a drugstore, the building became a grocery, barbershop, and dry cleaners before it assumed its present life as a private residence.

OPPOSITE, RIGHT: Christmas stockings created from white packing peanuts, adorned by snowflakes, and tied with white ribbons, are displayed on the wall.

ABOVE: A contemporary crystal chandelier designed by Chet hangs over the dining room table, which features a collection of more than two dozen candles of various sizes.

LEFT: A collection of candles casts a warm reflection on the marble dining room table.

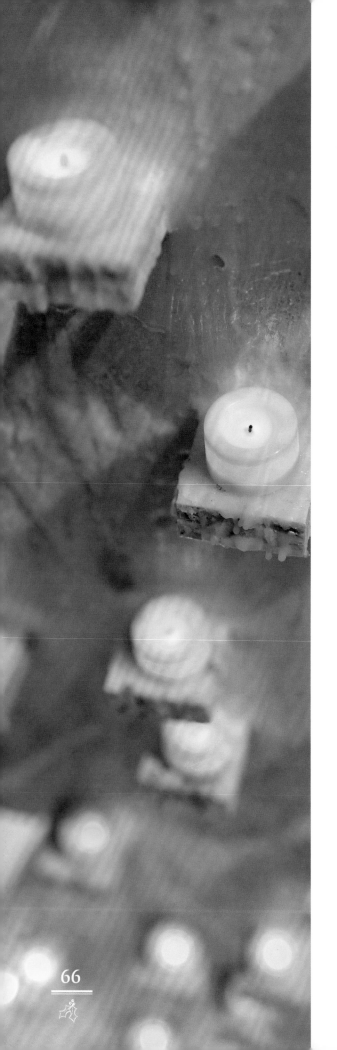

Chet definitely subscribes to the "more is better" philosophy when it comes to the use of candles. The marble-topped dining room table features more than two dozen candles of different sizes under a contemporary crystal chandelier that he designed, and three tiers of candles on an iron platform rest in front the wall of windows. "I feel the altar is very special since it was formerly used by St. Stephen Catholic Church on Napoleon Avenue," he says.

Chet and Jack moved into the house ten years ago. "When we found the place it was a rabbit's warren of

LEFT: Layers of wax were added to the plywood Christmas tree and the ledges that hold the battery-operated candles.

ABOVE: A black shelf topped with white candles, pine cones, and a tall bouquet of white twigs and branches greets you right inside the front door.

OPPOSITE: The white Christmas tree fashioned from plywood takes center stage in the living room.

tiny rooms," he says. Excited by the potential, they transformed it from an ugly duckling into a handsome prince of a house. "We opened up each room by adding French doors so all of the major spaces would have a view. We wanted each room to be connected to an outdoor patio, garden, or balcony."

Tiny white Christmas lights decorate all of the outdoor spaces during the holidays. "It does make it all look like a fairytale land," Chet says with a smile. "Yes, it's definitely correct to call it a 'white Christmas' home."

OPPOSITE: Even the bedroom gets special white holiday treatment with an oversized vase filled with twigs and branches on the glass table next to the easy chair and ottoman.

LEFT: A Mitchell Gaudet vase filled white twigs and branches is displayed on the table, while a cone-shaped vase by James Vella hangs on the wall.

TOP RIGHT: A variety of Origami paper animals decorates the twig Christmas tree in the dining room.

BOTTOM RIGHT: The late Christopher Maier carved the cabinet that features the torso of a man.

ALIX RICO

Designers' Holiday Magic

If Alix Rico's house could speak, it would speak

French. While many design professionals may embrace French influences and especially French antiques, Alix and Paul, her husband, truly are immersed in everything French, since they own a beautiful town house in the Luberon Valley in Provence. "We spend part of every year in our French home," Alix says with a smile. "It is here we have spent decades exploring the country looking for just the perfect French antiques and treasures to bring back to New Orleans for our clients and our annual sale."

Visiting the Ricos' home during the Christmas season will delight you if you are a Francophile. Every corner of each room seems to be chockablock with handsome French treasures such as angels, saints, antique candelabras, mirrors, paintings, and marvelous antique furniture. "I love to decorate, so Christmas is a nice time to 'overdo it' just a little bit," she says. "I try to celebrate the season with somewhat more of an over-the-top version of what I normally do."

Wander around this talented decorator's French-inspired holiday home, and you will quickly appreciate her style. "I always have white flowers and plants all over the house, and I enjoy adding seasonal trimmings to show the holiday spirit," she adds.

Instead of changing decorations each year, they develop through new additions. "Whenever I see something that would enhance or change my look in some way, I invest in it and save

OPPOSITE: A courtyard garden sets the European tone of the renovated 1940s cottage.

TOP RIGHT: An antique tabernacle, along with books, drawings, pomegranates, and holiday greens, create an interesting holiday tablescape in the foyer.

BOTTOM RIGHT: An angel, fresh flowers, winter bulbs in antique green pots from France, candles, and an old watering can welcome you at the front door.

it for the holidays," she answers. "I saw tiny lights on a wire in a shop at the beach one the summer and quickly bought them."

Alix loves interesting antique wooden pieces and never passes up anything that catches her eye. "Everything evolves over time, because although I love excess, I cannot abide clutter, so some things must be retired from time to time to add new finds."

One thing different about the Ricos' home at Christmas is that she never has a Christmas tree, Santa Claus, or red and green ribbons. "I prefer to pay homage to the season by things I personally love and admire. It is still traditional—just my brand of traditional."

The Ricos' house began life as a 1940s cottage. "When we found the house, it didn't have one attractive architectural element," Alix says. "However, it was on the right street, in the right neighborhood, and it was the right size. We purchased it ten years ago, did a complete renovation, and then Hurricane Katrina came, leaving four feet of water covering everything. This is a sad story to tell since we had just moved into the house the year before the hurricane." Not to be outdone, Alix and Paul rolled up their sleeves for a second complete renovation. "Since our last house was on the same street, you know we love the neighborhood, the live oak canopy, and the feeling of open space."

Today, the house is still picture perfect. "We definitely recaptured the handsome French face from our initial renovations," Alix adds. "We love the tall French doors

ABOVE: The large foyer is a study in exquisite French taste.

LEFT: A carved French archangel stands next to a polychrome Italian lamp in the living room. Wooden tassels, candles, and holiday greens complete the tablescape.

and windows that we added, and our oversized fireplace in the sitting room makes it extra cozy. We also enjoy how we made the old dining room a large foyer. The second renovation was heart breaking, but we tweaked many things to make them even better than before Katrina.

"It all feels very French to us, especially always having pots of blooming flowers around the tall double front doors." The many French touches the couple added to their house in both renovations adds to the spendor of their Christmas. "It always pleases me to see our house dressed for the holidays," Alix says. "The French really know how to celebrate Christmas, and we do, too."

ABOVE: White Christmas birds, on the Christopher Maier silver-leaf coffee table with an antique mirrored top in the living room, are part of the decorative theme throughout the house.

RIGHT: The mantel over the fireplace is Alix's interpretation of a white Christmas: white birds, white flowers, white birds, and white lights. Hungarian artist Bela Pallik painted the lambs over the fireplace.

HAL
WILLIAMSON

There is only one word

to describe Hal Williamson's Garden District home: magnificent. Stand at the front gate of the famous mansion at Fourth and Prytania Streets and marvel at its beauty. There isn't a mansion in New Orleans that can surpass the grandeur of the stately house that was built in 1859 by Col. Henry Short, a man who made his fortune as a commission merchant in the bustling antebellum cotton industry. Designed in the Italianate style by Henry Howard, a famous architect of the time, it is noted for its lovely cast-iron fence of cornstalks intertwined with morning glories.

Walk inside when the mansion is dressed in its Christmas finery, and be prepared to be charmed. "Christmastime has always been important in our lives and the lives of our families," explains interior decorator Hal, who has owned the house with Dr. Dale LeBlanc, his partner, since 1994. Preservationists at heart, the handsome men are perfect caretakers of the noted historic home, which always has been a gem in a neighborhood of many majestic antebellum mansions.

"We like to carry on the tradition of using all of our treasured family antique china, silver, and crystal that have been left to us by our favorite

TOP LEFT: The period Louis XVI sofa, from Lucullus Antiques in the French Quarter, is signed by the cabinet maker. Poinsettias fill the front of the fireplace, and antique Irish chandeliers are adorned with magnolia leaves. The stockings hung from the mantel were made by Hal's great-aunt Sara Malcom-Wright from Georgia.

TOP RIGHT: The historic 1859 mansion in the Garden District is noted for its unique cast-iron fence of cornstalks intertwined with morning glories.

BOTTOM LEFT: Hal and Dale call this tree the tree of memories because it is decorated with treasured ornaments the couple has collected since childhood. The Eiffel Tower ornament was purchased on a trip to Paris.

great-aunts and great grandparents to entertain our family and friends," Hal says. "We both have similar Southern traditions that we uphold as way of connecting us back to happy childhood memories, when our grandparents used to entertain on a grand scale. So we carry these traditions forward in hopes that the generation coming along today will have as wonderful memories as we did."

A tall Fraser Fir or Noble Fir gets the nod for the Christmas tree to reach to the top

ABOVE: The grand piano in the music room was made the same year the house was built (1859). Hal's workroom made the Bayou-green silk taffeta drapes.

LEFT: Draped in magnolia garland and accented with oranges, kumquats, and tangerine silk ribbon, the marble mantel in the dining room is original to the home. Louis Philippe "Vieux Paris" urns are topped with pineapples, a symbol of hospitality.

OPPOSITE: The tall Christmas tree is placed in the reading room. It is decorated with sentimental ornaments that have been collected over a lifetime.

of the sixteen-foot ceilings. "We always place the tree in the reading area that is decorated with French Empire antique furniture," Hal says. "We call our tree the tree of memories, because we decorate it with treasured ornaments we have both collected since childhood. There are ornaments from a brother, parent, friend, or maybe just something that we found in our travels together. To make the tree sparkle, we use lots of twinkling lights. The end result is Christmas tree that makes us very happy."

One of the couple's main Christmas traditions is having their main meal on Christmas day in the early afternoon. "It allows the family not to rush in the morning and to have time to go to church," he says. Fourteen chairs around the elegantly dressed dining room table and a second table seating six nearby accommodate the twenty that enjoy the grand Christmas meal, which always includes gumbo made by Dale's mother.

"Our menu is usually the same: smoked turkey and ham, sweet potatoes baked with oranges, asparagus and English pea casserole, Southern-style cornbread dressing, and giblet gravy, with a side dish of orange-cranberry relish." It is expected that the meal-goers over-indulge on desserts with Dale's grandmother Daisy's coconut cake, Hal's grandmother's caramel cake, a French Yule log, pecan pies, ambrosia, and homemade cookies and pralines.

"Yes, we do know how to enjoy Christmas is this marvelous house," Hal says. "We love the many traditions we have created. We like to be reminded of happy times, so we do not change how we decorate from year to year or how we open our doors to share the a happy season with our family and friends."

ABOVE: A second table seating six is nestled in the bay window of the dining room to provide extra seating for the grand Christmas meal.

OPPOSITE, LEFT: Petit fours and cookies are offered on a pair of tiered antique stands.

OPPOSITE, TOP RIGHT: A coconut cake from Dale's mother's grandmother's recipe and a caramel cake from Hal's grandmother's recipe are dessert stars of the Christmas meal.

OPPOSITE, CENTER RIGHT: A sweet potato pie awaits holiday guests.

OPPOSITE, BOTTOM RIGHT: The rich French Yule log is a regular dessert offering at Christmastime.

BEAUREGARD-KEYES HOUSE

Historic Homes

Walk up the winding steps to the historic

OPPOSITE: **The Jacobean furniture in the dining room, acquired by Frances Parkinson Keyes from Uncle Sam's plantation on River Road, dates to the early 1800s.**

BELOW: **Located at 1113 Chartres Street in the French Quarter, the Beauregard-Keyes House was built in 1826. Throughout its history, two of its significant occupants left their names on the building: Gen. P. G. T. Beauregard, a noted Confederate leader, and Francis Parkinson Keyes, a famous novelist.**

Beauregard-Keyes House on Chartres Street in the French Quarter at Christmastime and enter the storybook of a Victorian mansion. Built in 1826 by Joseph Le Carpentier, a well-to-do auctioneer, "the house is decorated as it would have been during the 1860s when Gen. Pierre Gustav Toutant Beauregard, a noted Confederate leader who hailed from Louisiana, lived in it," explains Larry Schmidt, the executive director of the Beauregard-Keyes House. "Visitors can still enjoy the simplicity of the decorations that highlights the stunning architecture. It is easy to be transported to a time long ago when the Christmas season was honored and celebrated."

The rich history of the house is well documented, yet only two names of former residents remain on the building today: that of a Confederate general, P. G. T. Beauregard, and that of a noted author, Frances Parkinson Keyes. General Beauregard is a legendary Civil War hero, and—from all accounts—Keyes lived a robust life writing best-selling books and entertaining in a well-fitting grand manor.

History records that when Keyes first came to Louisiana, she simply rented the house and settled in her routine, becoming a prolific writer along the way. Later, Keyes decided to purchase the house and employed skilled restoration architects and workmen to transform the house into the stately edifice it is today. The Keyes Foundation was formed in 1948 and entrusted to the care of the building.

Open to the public on a regular basis, the holiday season is an ideal time for a visit. "All of the decorations are historically accurate and handmade by the staff and

board members," says Ella Camburnbeck, the enthusiastic house director. She smiles as she reads from an article about Christmas decorations of the period from an 1860 issue of *Godey's Magazine,* also known as *Godey's Magazine and Lady's Book,* which was the most popular magazine in the country at the time with a circulation of 150,000: "Christmas decorations include strings of bright berries, small bouquets of paper flowers, strings of beads, tiny flags of gray ribbons, stars and shields of gilt paper, lace bags filled with colored candies, and knots of bright ribbon, all homemade."

ABOVE: A Nativity scene has a place of honor on the mantel in the ballroom.

LEFT: Fruit was always part a part in decorating for the holidays in the nineteenth century.

OPPOSITE: Gen. P. G. T. Beauregard's portrait has a place of honor over the fireplace, while his first wife Marie Laure Villere's portrait hangs nearby. Both resided in the home.

PREVIOUS PAGE: The light-filled room across from the ballroom was used as a library by Francis Parkinson Keyes, a noted author who lived in the house from 1944 until she died in 1970.

ABOVE: The Christmas tree, featuring ornaments of the period, is displayed in the center of the room under the antique chandelier.

OPPOSITE, LEFT: The 1870 piano has been played for the pleasure of the residents of the house and their guests for more than a century.

OPPOSITE, RIGHT: A painted egg delights as a Christmas ornament.

There's a joyful spirit in the holiday face of the Beauregard-Keyes House today. Dolls of the period sit at low tables in a corner of the parlor having tea and desserts, and even one tiny tea set is decorated with Christmas trees. Nun dolls sit in antique chairs, paying homage to the Ursuline order that already existed across the street when the house was built.

A Christmas tree is on view in front of the fireplace and directly under the antique chandelier. Decorated with treasures from the past, the tree sits on an antique marble-topped table. Of special note are the paper cones filled with nuts and small candies that hang from the tree by colorful ribbons. A lace angel is perched at the very top, and fruit is interspersed on the branches below.

An antique piano nearby is seemingly just waiting for a lady in period costume to play Christmas carols. Fresh fruit and ribbons atop the piano further add to the spirited feeling of the Christmas season. French doors in the parlor open onto a balcony.

A grand dining room joins the parlor at the rear of the house, furnished with fine antiques and accessories. The holiday spirit continues with fresh fruit placed in the center of the table, giving the stately mansion the look—and smell—of Christmas.

GALLIER
HOUSE

Historic Homes

Gallier House sits majestically

at 1132 Royal Street, a marvel of a bygone era when James Gallier Jr., the most prominent New Orleans architect of his day, designed and built the classic house for his family in 1860. Today, the historic house-turned-museum shares all of the beauty of the past with the public, particularly during the holiday season, when the home displays traditional nineteenth-century decorations. "There is no better time to visit Gallier House than during December," explains Mamie Sterkx Gasperecz, executive director of the home, which is listed in the National Register of Historic Places and as a National Historic Landmark. "The holiday decorations provide a first-hand glimpse of how a New Orleans family like the Galliers would have celebrated the holiday season."

Step inside Gallier House's magnificent, large parlor, and you will journey back in time—great care has been taken to authentically recreate everything as it once was in this historic treasure. Of special interest is the Christmas tree decorated with egg cups painted gold and embellished with ribbons, hand-crocheted snowflakes, and fabric ornaments. Occasionally lit on the tree are small white candles. It isn't a floor-to-ceiling tree common in homes today but rather simple and small. Yet, there is something truly beautiful in its simplicity.

Other holiday decorations in the room include the silver-tiered stands of seasonal fruit centered on the round tables, with candy treats featured on the dual lower arms. The original black marble mantels are dressed with pine cones and branches, fresh fruit, and

TOP LEFT: The grand parlor is a study of elegance with greenery and fruit used to decorate for the Christmas season.

TOP RIGHT: Completed in 1860, Gallier House was built by the well-known architect James Gallier Jr. for his family's residence.

BOTTOM RIGHT: The original iron gates were designed by James Gallier Jr.

89

greenery flowing from the fine porcelain vases. Also on display are the intricate cones of fabric and paper filled with nuts, a holiday treat typically given to guests or young children.

One interesting architectural note is that Gallier designed a single parlor rather than the usual double parlors divided by pocket doors that were the fashion of the day. Instead, he added interesting gold-topped columns to provide the feeling of double parlors. Then, to further add to the grandeur of the space, he had elaborate moldings fashioned around the room. The fine furnishings, elaborate drapes, and authentic artwork in the house are exhibited in a similar manner as when the Galliers lived in the house.

The nearby dining room with its grandly appointed table appears to be ready for a holiday meal. Here again fruit plays an important part in the holiday decorations, with a bowl of fruit displayed in the center of the table and oranges interspersed with greenery on the sideboard.

OPPOSITE: The grandeur of the parlor is showcased with the round table in the foreground set with a silver epergne holding fruit at the top and candy featured on the two bottom arms.

TOP: The furnishings of Gallier House are authentic to the period. Lemons and pine branches decorate the top of the table under the painting.

BOTTOM LEFT: Pine branches and lemons decorate the top of chest in the parlor.

BOTTOM RIGHT: Greenery fills the porcelain vase on the mantel, which is decorated with pinecones, evergreen braches, and a pomegranate.

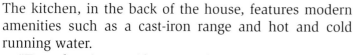

The kitchen, in the back of the house, features modern amenities such as a cast-iron range and hot and cold running water.

"To authenticate mid-century decorations and holiday life, we turned to the pages of publications of the day such as *Peterson's Ladies National Magazine,* a popular publication that focused on women, as well as diaries and prints from the period," Gasperecz says. "To dress

LEFT: Example of food that may have been served for a holiday meal is shown on the dining room table.

TOP RIGHT: A porcelain teacup with a slice of orange on the sideboard is ready for service.

BOTTOM RIGHT: A gold and crystal bowl filled with oranges and nut-stuffed cones graces the top of the small, marble-topped table.

OPPOSITE: The dining room table is prepared for a grand holiday meal.

ABOVE: The kitchen features a cast-iron stove fitted into the fireplace.

BOTTOM LEFT: A basket waits atop a chair, ready to be delivered to a needy family as a Christmas gift.

BOTTOM RIGHT: The mirrored display cabinet in the dining room holds the dessert crème pots, while homemade candy is displayed in the nearby compote.

the Christmas tree, we used information from the 1858 *New Orleans Daily Crescent,* the local newspaper of the day."

Celebrating Christmas in New Orleans has always been an important part of the mostly Catholic city. Taking a step into the world of a historic New Orleans Christmas by visiting Gallier House simply adds to the joy of the holiday season.

ABOVE: At the base of the Christmas tree, a doll of the period sits with other small gifts and toys.

RIGHT: Small cornucopias holding nuts, made from fabric and paper, were used as a gift when guests came to call.

HERMANN-GRIMA HOUSE

Historic Homes

Hermann-Grima House at 820

St. Louis Street in the French Quarter has much to share during the holiday season. The historic house built in 1831, all dressed up in its Christmas finery, offers a holiday hearth cooking demonstration. Each week, volunteers work in the authentic kitchen, preparing food as it would have been done in the 1830s. "It is amazing to watch the dedicated volunteers cook over an open fire in the hearth kitchen," explains Mamie Sterkx Gasperecz, executive director of the house, which is uniquely Federal by design. "The Creole cooking demonstrations feature interesting dishes such as Louisiana navel orange compote, cranberry walnut bread, and cornbread rolls."

The kitchen is part of the detached building at the rear of the house that includes the original slave quarters. There are four main ways to cook: over the hearth fire, down hearth (complete with short-legged grill and spider pots), in the beehive oven, and in stew holes (a brick surface with cavities capable of simmering gumbos, stews, and red beans). Of special interest is the courtyard citrus garden, maintained as it would have been when Marie Emeranthe Becnel and Samuel Hermann, the original owners, occupied the house.

Hermann was a wealthy commodities broker who hired Virginia architect and builder William Brand to design and construct the home. The end result more closely resembles the architecture of the mid-Atlantic and northeastern United States than the French- and Spanish-inspired architecture common in early nineteenth-century New Orleans.

RIGHT: Built in 1831, the Hermann-Grima historic house museum takes on a special glow at Christmas, when it is decorated in keeping with the period of its construction.

ABOVE: The grand dining room table is decorated with a cone-shaped apple display in the center with pears, apples, and oranges around the base. The silk-damask drapes are reproduction of a pattern popular in the 1830s.

RIGHT: A pinecone rests near two nineteenth-century books in the library.

Today, the property is known as the Hermann-Grima House because the Hermanns only lived on the property until 1844, when it was sold to Felix Grima. Grima, a lawyer and judge, along with Adelaide, his wife, and their nine children lived in the house until 1921.

Holiday decorations in the house are in keeping with how a grand mansion would have been dressed in nineteenth-century New Orleans. Persimmons and sour oranges, fresh from the

97

Hermann-Grima garden, were always liberally used in holiday decorations, as were fresh holiday greens.

"Christmas trees as we know them today were not in existence when the Hermann family moved into their new mansion," Gasperecz says. "It was not until the widely circulated picture of Queen Victoria's family tree in an 1848 edition of the *London Illustrated News* that Christmas trees became widely used, with one of the earliest documentations of a Christmas tree in New Orleans appearing in the *New Orleans Daily Crescent* of 1858."

ABOVE: The parlor is complete with a portrait of Marie Virginie Hermann by Jean Joseph Vaudechamp. Red silk damask drapes and upholstery, typical of the 1830s, add elegance to the room.

LEFT: The unique round mirror holds four candles. Compotes of fruit are displayed on the table.

OPPOSITE, TOP: The Brussels carpet in the parlor and dining room was made in England and loomed in twenty-seven-inch strips. A portrait of Marie Virginie Hermann hangs over the piano in the front parlor.

OPPOSITE, BOTTOM: A portrait of Marie Emeranthe Hermann is displayed over the dessert table.

Christmas Eve in most New Orleans homes was a time of religious observance. After midnight mass at St. Louis Cathedral, the families enjoyed a late night supper called the réveillon. At the Hermann home, the handsome dining room was the scene for the grand meal, with decorations for the occasion featuring a cone fashioned of apples in the center of the table and greenery on the fireplace mantels. The food was cooked in the outdoor hearth kitchen and then brought into the butler's pantry, transferred onto the fine serving pieces, and brought to the table.

ABOVE: The hearth kitchen is part of the detached building in the rear courtyard. It features a large fireplace, beehive oven, and stew holes (a brick-surfaced cavity capable of simmering gumbos, stews, and red beans). All of the food on the table was prepared in the kitchen.

RIGHT: The storage in the kitchen displays typical tools, utensils, and ingredients of the time.

OPPOSITE: The library has a Christmas wreath in the window and holly on the desk.

The non-profit Woman's Exchange operates the Hermann-Grima House along with Gallier House. "Our goal is to preserve, maintain, and complete the restoration of the properties, to interpret their place in and contribution to the culture of New Orleans, and to educate visitors about the history of New Orleans and its population in the period of 1830 to 1880," Gasperecz proudly explains. A visit to New Orleans during the Christmas season is greatly enhanced by enjoying the historical houses and museum.

OPPOSITE: Traditional holiday dishes prepared in the hearth kitchen. *Creole Cooking*, published in 1885 by the Christian Woman's Exchange, was one of the first cookbooks published on the subject. Many of the dishes prepared in the hearth kitchen are taken from the book.

TOP LEFT: Roast veal and garlic on a bed of fresh parsley.

BOTTOM LEFT: Plum pudding with candied fruit.

RIGHT: Holiday rolls baked in the beehive oven.

LONGUE VUE HOUSE AND GARDENS

Historic Homes

Longue Vue House and Gardens at 7 Bamboo

Road is a suburban oasis, unlike the four other house museums in New Orleans, which are all located in the French Quarter. Surrounded by eight acres of magnificent gardens, the home was designed by brothers Geoffrey and William Platt and completed in 1942, making it the only historic museum home in the area built in the twentieth century. Ellen Biddle Shipman, a renowned landscape architect of the day, created the gardens and interior design.

OPPOSITE: Located at 7 Bamboo Road, Longue Vue House and Gardens is a treasured house and garden museum that is open to the public. At Christmastime, it is decorated both inside and out, reminiscent of the years when it was the home of Edith and Edgar Stern, who created the eight-acre estate. The west façade is based on Palladian design.

"Edith and Edgar Stern created Longue Vue, an architectural masterpiece that seamlessly integrates indoor and outdoor spaces, which is one of the finest house-garden museums in the country today," explains Tony Chauveaux, executive director of Longue Vue House and Gardens. "It is open to the public for all seasons of the year, yet no time is more perfect than Christmas, when the home is decorated for the holiday season. And, for *lagniappe,* you can even come to one of our special holiday teas."

No expense was spared to furnish the twenty-room home in the finest English and American antiques, European and Eastern European carpets, and modern and contemporary art. The Sterns were well-known patrons of local artists as well as collectors of the masters of their day. Also of note is the couple's collection of Chinese and European export porcelain, Staffordshire transferware,

LEFT: The *Three Grace Fountain* was bought by Edgar on Royal Street in 1951. Holiday decorations on the exterior of Longue Vue House include swags of greenery tied with large red bows draped on the doorway and balcony. Fresh flowers in clay pots are grouped around the doorway to add to the festive mood.

and creamware and pearlware from Wedgwood.

The four-story, 22,000-square foot Classic Revival residence's holiday dress is in keeping with decorations the Sterns would have displayed. Even the unique exterior, featuring four distinct façades, each one with its own garden, is dressed for the holiday season in greenery tied with red bows draped around the doors on both the first and second floors, as well as the balcony. Fresh flowers growing in clay pots line the steps and add a festival mood as you enter the house.

Red and white poinsettias are used throughout the interior of the house, which is furnished with fine antiques. Mantels are adorned with fresh fruit and greenery, and a tall Christmas tree

ABOVE: The large dining room was the scene of grand holiday meals. A separate dessert table is positioned in the bay window. The wallpaper is made from a series of Chinese rice paper screens, which had decorated Ellen Shipman's own dining room in her New York City home before being installed at Longue Vue.

LEFT: Of special note is the Bohemian ruby-red crystal stemware that was inherited by Edith Stern from her parents.

OPPOSITE: Red, pink, and white poinsettias add to the holiday spirit on the colonnade that joins the main residence with the Playhouse.

graces the lower hall next to the winding stairway, an architectural work of art. The tree is decorated with glass ornaments from the 1940s and 50s, as well as multi-colored lights and baubles, and red poinsettias completely rim the bottom of the tree. Greenery tied with large red bows adorns the stairway, which ends with a tower of apples topped by a pineapple affixed to the bottom of the banister. In recognition of their Jewish heritage, a Chanukah display has a place of honor on the trestle table in the lower hall.

Since the Sterns loved to entertain, the dining room takes on a particular elegance during the holiday season. The table features Bohemian ruby red crystal stemware, inherited by Edith from her parents, which was often used during the holiday season. Adding to the festive mood, red poinsettias fill the front of the fireplace. A

ABOVE: A large Christmas tree has a place of honor next to the stairway on the first level. Red poinsettias circle the tree, and magnolia branches tied with red bows adorn the stairway. A unique tower of apples topped by a pineapple rests atop the banister at the bottom of the stairway.

OPPOSITE, TOP: The top of the doorway to the gallery is decorated with fresh fruit and magnolia leaves.

OPPOSITE, BOTTOM LEFT: The white ceramic tree is one of a pair that had special meaning to Edith Stern because they were given to her by friends.

OPPOSITE, BOTTOM RIGHT: A holiday arrangement in the upper hall includes red berries.

pair of small white ceramic Christmas trees from the Twentieth Century Shop on St. Charles Avenue is incorporated in the dining room decorations.

While much can be said about the interesting interior of Longue Vue, it is the gardens that draw many of the visitors to the treasured National Historic Landmark. Shipman had a flair for both the formal and natural elements she brought to Longue Vue. Fortunately, with the usual mild winters of the area, something is always blooming, and a holiday season visit is sure to make you want to visit during the other three seasons.

OPPOSITE: The second-floor view of the three-story winding stairway is decorated for Christmas with magnolia branches tied with gold-tipped red bows.

ABOVE: The Wedgewood-blue color of the room gives it a special coziness. Fine antiques and a painting titled *Several Circles*, by Wassily Kandinsky, adds to the charm of the house.

RIGHT: In keeping with the holiday spirit, red poinsettias are positioned in front of the fireplace in the dining room.

WILLIAMS
RESIDENCE

Historic Homes

The home of Gen. L.

Kemper and Leila Hardie Moore Williams at 718 Toulouse Street in the French Quarter is one the five treasured museum houses in New Orleans that offers a glimpse of Christmas past for the public to enjoy during the holiday season. Built in 1889 as home for the Trapolin family, it was acquired in 1938 by General and Mrs. Williams as their private residence. Today, the museum house is part of The Historic New Orleans Collection (THNOC), established as a non-profit foundation by the Williams couple, who had amassed a substantial collection of important Louisiana materials that they felt merited public access.

"The staff and volunteers enjoy dressing up the house with Christmas decorations that were popular in the 1950s and reflect Leila Williams's elegant style," explains Priscilla Lawrence, executive director of THNOC. "Since Kemper and Leila Williams did not have children of their own, they held family celebrations with all of their nieces and nephews. Old family photographs from 1956 through 1961 are also displayed during the holiday season, giving visitors a glimpse into the Williams' traditions. The Christmas tree is decorated every year using some of the original pinecone ornaments."

The 3,938-square-foot Williams Residence was built with an Italianate façade and rooms opening *en suite* (one after another, or, in sequence). It has an elaborate ironwork balcony topped by fan lights with a series of French doors that opens onto a brick courtyard. Holiday decorations include myriad red poinsettias in clay pots lining the stairway with red bows topping the cone-shaped greenery at the main entrance. The side and rear courtyards are also dressed with poinsettias, wreaths, and garland.

TOP LEFT: A large Christmas tree is displayed in the corner of the living room. It is mostly decorated with keepsake ornaments from the time of Leila and Kemper Williams.

TOP RIGHT: Built in 1889, the exterior of the Williams Residence is decorated with red poinsettias and green wreaths hung with red ribbon tied into large bows for the holidays.

113

Inside the elegant drawing room, it looks much as it did when the Williams were in residence. A large Christmas tree, almost touching the ceiling, fills the corner of the room. It is decorated with many of the same ornaments that the Williams couple would have used. Fine antiques and comfortable seating is provided in the large room that has three tall French doors topped with fan lights that open onto a private courtyard. Red poinsettias have a place of honor in front of the fireplace, while the mirror over the mantel provides an interesting reflection of the Christmas tree.

In the intimate dining room, the table is dressed for a grand meal. While it was the custom of the day not to include flowers in the center of the dining room table, red poinsettias in front of the tall windows give the room a festive holiday look. It is easy to imagine Kemper and Leila Williams entertaining their extended family for a grand meal in this elegant room.

ABOVE: Dressed for a grand meal, the dining room features the original table settings that belonged to Leila and Kemper Williams.

RIGHT: The Christmas tree is decorated with ornaments such as the white ball in the foreground.

FAR RIGHT: A classic iron lamppost stands in the center of the side courtyard. A wreath of greenery fashioned with a red bow decorates the lamppost.

OPPOSITE: Rooftops of French Quarter buildings are evidenced just over the wall that provides privacy for the side courtyard.

Large windows in the upstairs bedroom overlooking the courtyard can be pushed up to become doors, giving access to the balcony. Once again, poinsettias play an important roll in paying respect to the holiday season.

Although the Williams home has a place of importance as part of The Historic New Orleans Collection, it is important to note that in addition to being a museum and research center, the Collection publishes books dedicated to the study and preservation of the history and culture of New Orleans and the Gulf South region.

In the more than forty years since its founding, THNOC has greatly added to its historical holdings and augmented the physical structures that house them, established ambitious publishing and exhibition schedules, and added approximately 350,000 photographs, prints, drawings, paintings, and other artifacts to its collections.

OPPOSITE: **An important map of New Orleans hangs on the wall of the hallway between the parlor and dining room.**

ABOVE: **The upstairs bedroom overlooks the courtyard through walk-out windows that open onto a balcony.**

RIGHT: **The mirror over the mantel in the living room provides an interesting reflection of the large Christmas tree.**

POE AND GUY CARPENTER

Garden District Enchantment

The stately home of Poe and Guy

Carpenter on Third Street in the Garden District was built in 1870 by William Herndon Hogan. It incorporates both Italianate and Greek Revival elements such as the Corinthian columns in the Greek Revival style and Italianate windows, doors, paired brackets, and ornamental iron railings. The stately home is always tastefully dressed for the holiday season. "For the exterior, we always use garland tied with red bows on the balcony, and each window is festooned with a wreath tied with a red ribbon," Poe says.

She is quick to point out since there are three children—Cook, Chase and Chloe—at home, the elegant house lends itself to a casual lifestyle. Step inside the amazing forty-foot-long kitchen that Guy, a contractor and owner of Supreme Restoration LLC, fashioned at the end of the side hall, and you can imagine the laughter and happy voices that fill the room during the holidays. "Yes, the kitchen is always the gathering place for our family and the friends, and especially the friends of our children," Poe quickly adds. "I love that

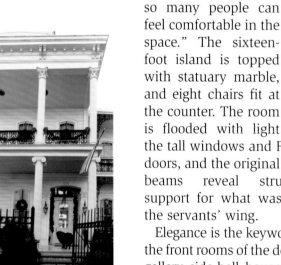

so many people can feel comfortable in the space." The sixteen-foot island is topped with statuary marble, and eight chairs fit at the counter. The room is flooded with light from the tall windows and French doors, and the original wood beams reveal structural support for what was once the servants' wing.

Elegance is the keyword for the front rooms of the double-gallery side-hall house, with the front parlor awash with neutral tones of cream and off-white. It features a pair

ABOVE: The forty-foot long kitchen features a sixteen-foot island topped with statuary marble.

LEFT: Built in 1870, the Garden District home was purchased by Poe and Guy Carpenter in 2007.

OPPOSITE: Artist Clay Judice Jr. from Lafayette did the drawing of Cook, Chloe, and Chase that hangs in the front hallway.

of sofas covered in white linen, with a table from Kathy Slater Interiors on Magazine Street in the center. The original antique pine floors are covered with a tightly woven brown rug topped by a cowhide to further define the seating area. "The mirror over the fireplace is original to the house." Poe says. "For the holidays, we keep the mantel dressed simply with greens and pair of white Christmas trees on one side and angels on the other end." To complete the pared down yet dramatic look, the couple purchased an antique chandelier from Mac Maison, also on Magazine Street, to hang in the center of the room.

"We love to put our tall Christmas tree in the nook next to the second parlor, where it doesn't interrupt the flow of traffic from room to room," Poe continues. "I wanted this room to have more of a casual feeling. I didn't want anyone to be afraid to sit down and relax—kids included. After all, there's a television over the fireplace." Adding colorful draperies fashioned by Renee LeJeune Laborde provides a cheerful look to the room, which has glass holiday balls on the mantel and in a bowl behind the sofa. A matching chandelier to the

TOP: With the Christmas tree placed in a niche just off the second parlor, it isn't in the way of traffic, yet it can be viewed from both rooms.

BOTTOM: The elegant dining room showcases the house's elaborate original molding.

one in the front parlor helps unify the two spaces.

The grand dining room across from the front parlor is illuminated by an antique chandelier from New Orleans Auction Gallery. "It would be nice to say that we always have grand holiday meals in the dining room," Poe adds with a smile. "In all honesty, sometime we just eat in the kitchen."

The festive holiday spirit continues on the back porch, where the family enjoys gathering. "With our mild winters, we love to use the porch for entertaining from time to time around the holidays," she says. Here, you will find red poinsettias on the green iron furniture and on the tables nearby in the seating area under the fan.

"When we bought this house in 2007, we wanted to be ever respectful of its historical significance, yet make it a comfortable in every sense of the word, and that's exactly what we have done. Today it is an ideal family home."

ABOVE: When the weather permits, the couple enjoys entertaining on the back porch.

RIGHT: A pair of sofas face each other in front of the fireplace in the elegant living room. The tall mirror is original to the house, while the antique chandelier was acquired from Mac Maison on Magazine Street.

121

JANE MULLALLY CROSS

Garden District Enchantment

Jane Mullally Cross grins as

she says, "I always put my Christmas tree on the front porch. It may be the only home in the Garden District with a tree on the front porch, but the tree in the house makes my allergies act up, so out it goes on the front porch."

There is something charming about discovering a Christmas tree on the front porch of such a grand mansion, and Jane's house is definitely charming. The parlor welcomes visitors with colorful, terra cotta-colored walls and twin sofas and bold yellow drapes in the same material featuring tobacco leaves covering the large windows. Pocket doors lead to the library.

For holiday decorations, the mantel in the parlor is topped with candles, greenery, and Christmas baubles that are also used on the nearby dining room mantel. "You won't find the usual holiday decoration in the house," Jane says. "It isn't my style to be like everybody else. The house itself doesn't need to be overdressed for Christmas—we take it easy and all gather together to share the joy of Christmas."

The light-filled house captures the beauty of a historic mansion without being "fussy." Even the plaid drapes in the dining room seem to have a playful quality about them. Yes, there's a grand Waterford chandelier hanging over the dining room table and an oil portrait of a relative over the fireplace, but on an opposite wall there's a contemporary painting, and the corner of the room is filled with live plants that thrive in the light from the big windows. Nothing is boring in this house, not even the pillows that line the sofa in the family room, which are fashioned in five different colors.

There's a lot to be said about the pedigree of the house. It was designed by Henry Howard, one of the leading architects of the

day, and completed in 1844. Jane and James Darcy were the first owners, and even their names seem to denote they were a couple of importance in their day, rather like characters in a Jane Austin novel.

The curved windows on the front of the house and the cast-iron railings on the galleries are reminiscent of the Italianate style, while the Corinthian columns that frame the front are Greek Revival, as is the roofline. Sheltered by the attic room is a very large, built-in dollhouse that was made for Jane's daughter when she was a young girl. In her day, she would even decorate the dollhouse for Christmas.

ABOVE: An antique Waterford crystal chandelier hangs over the table in the dining room.

RIGHT: The tall Christmas tree on the front porch almost touches the ceiling.

OPPOSITE: Built in 1844, the Garden District mansion on Second Street has been the home of Jane Mullally Cross since the 1974.

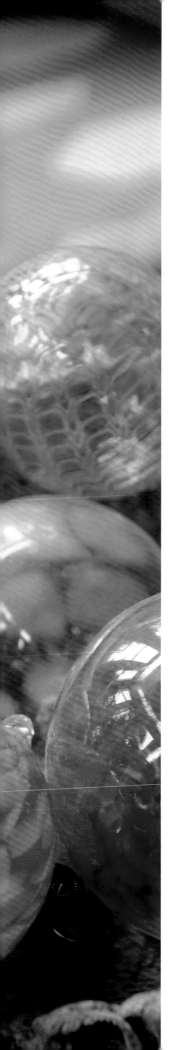

There is also the story about Lottie Miller, a kindergarten teacher who lived and ran a school in the house. She was described by the local newspaper as "the epitome of Southern culture and manners, intelligent, quiet, gracious, with a sense of humor, and infinite understanding of her pupils, her steady blue eyes, and a look enough to keep the most obstreperous girl in line." The school grew to include the kindergarten through twelfth grades. In 1931, after graduating her last class, Miss Miller sold the house.

Jane tends to her own garden that is a storybook vision of jasmine, hibiscus, and trumpet plants skirting the rear courtyard. When the holiday weather is

ABOVE: **A comfortable library just off the front parlor is a quiet spot for reading.**

BELOW: **An antique painting of men playing pool hangs over the mantel, which is decorated with candles, colorful Christmas baubles, and greenery.**

OPPOSITE, LEFT: **Simple holiday decorating on the sun porch is executed by adding a bowl of colorful glass balls.**

OPPOSITE, TOP: **Warm terra cotta-colored walls add warmth to the parlor, with the pair of sofas and the draperies covered in matching bold yellow, patterned fabric featuring tobacco leaves.**

OPPOSITE, BOTTOM: **An antique table in the hallway is decorated with silver angels, greenery, and candles.**

warm, the laughter of her ten grandchildren fills the air of the courtyard and garden. "I love when my entire extended family is here for the holidays," she says, reminiscing that she has lived in the house since 1974. "This house loves to be filled with family and friends celebrating the joys of Christmas together."

OPPOSITE: Overlooking the garden, the sun porch is furnished with white wicker furniture and colorful cushions and pillows.

ABOVE: The family room is flooded with light from the tall French doors, which make up an entire wall.

LEFT: Fresh fruit and roses provide simple holiday decorations in the family room.

SHAUN AND FOSTER DUNCAN

Garden District Enchantment

Some homes in the Garden District sit tall and

imposing, poster children for the historic mansions you see in movies. Others are almost hidden behind thick hedges, iron gates, and fences that make you wonder if there is a secret garden out of view. Stop for a moment at the home of Shaun and Foster Duncan, and take the time to look into the garden of their Camp Street home. "Aren't we fortunate to enjoy green gardens at Christmastime, when we can plant narcissus and amaryllis, accented by yellow spikes of ligularia?" asks Shaun. "What a natural complement to the garland, lights, and ribbon bows. Our garden neatly hugs the L-shape of our house, and we enjoy the privacy yet the connection to street life." Landscape architect Doug Reed of Reed Hilderbrand in Cambridge, Massachusetts, emphasized the connection of the house to the courtyard and garden. His design incorporates newly installed brick steps with reconfigured planting beds.

The charming home, nestled on a narrow lot, began its humble origins circa 1830 as a horse stable. It isn't exactly known when the present house was built, but today it is a comfortable home and architectural gem. "We do know that architect Pio Lyons designed the new living room and library at the rear of the house in 1976 for Susan and Clancy Dupepe," Shaun says. The new addition fits perfectly with the historical part of the house, since great care was taken to add old ceiling beams, wide plank floors, antique wood for the mantels, and fireplace surrounds. Even the old wood used for paneling in library helps to give everything a special, aged patina.

When the Duncans purchased the home in 2011, they had Michael Carbine design and build a new entrance vestibule. Later,

OPPOSITE: An antique chandelier adorned with Italian papier mâché angels hangs from the vaulted ceiling in the dining room. A Chinese ancestral portrait on the wall is illuminated by a pair of silver lamps topped with Florentine shades.

BELOW: The elegant Garden District home of Shaun and Foster Duncan began life around 1830 as a horse stable. Today, it is an architectural gem with a pristine garden.

they enclosed the side gallery to create a hallway leading to the private master suite. The layer of improvements to the home by each previous owner tells the stories of Garden District homes.

The Christmas season is joyful for the Duncan family—it's when daughter Katherine comes home from Philadelphia and son William, a student at Dartmouth College, is in town. "It is so lively when we are all together for the holidays," Shaun says. "I enjoy decorating the tree and the house with our collected family ornaments, many of which signify the children's interests, schools, and other cities where we have lived. Our crèche is always a part our holiday display since it was given piece by piece over Katherine's youth by my late mother."

During the holidays at the Duncans' home, the kitchen is always open and stocked with lace cookies and eggnog. "We welcome our friends and the children's friends over anytime—day, night, or early morning—and while the house has a unique and striking dining room with a vaulted cathedral ceiling, exposed beams, and a grand antique chandelier, much of our entertaining is done in a more informal manner."

TOP LEFT: Ceramic tiles collected over the years flank the decorative iron piece over the mantel in the kitchen.

TOP RIGHT: Lemon branches loaded with lemons are displayed on the mantel in the kitchen

OPPOSITE, TOP: White narcissus plants grow in front of a cherub to add interest in the side garden.

OPPOSITE, CENTER: The fountain in the side garden is the center of interest.

OPPOSITE, BOTTOM: The secret garden is hidden from the street by a mix of camellias and taxus.

OPPOSITE, RIGHT: A flowering amaryllis plant adds to the holiday feeling in the garden.

130

ABOVE: **Furnished in fine antiques, the sitting room features a four-panel stylized painting of an elephant with riders on multiple levels.**

OPPOSITE, TOP LEFT: **The eighteen-century English gilt-wood console with a marble top displays a pair of gilded Christmas angels, an Indonesian carved wooden boat with tribesmen, a glass bowl by artist Chaffe McIlhenny, and a colorful sculpture by the late John Scott. The painting above the table is by Nicole Charbonnet.**

OPPOSITE, BOTTOM LEFT: **Kitty Duncan, Foster's mother, made the stockings displayed on the marble mantel in the sitting room. The late New Orleans artist John Scott created the sculpture over the fireplace.**

OPPOSITE, BOTTOM RIGHT: **A garland of fresh greens tied with beaded ribbon bows is draped on the banister.**

The house has some important antiques, many of them chosen under the guidance of the late Leon Irwin, a noted arbiter of good taste. He found the rug in the living room at an auction sourced from an old plantation home. Some selections for their current home were made by interior designer Jeanne Barousse.

"We are both from New Orleans, so it was a happy homecoming to return to the city where we have so many relatives and friends after being away for thirteen years living in Louisville, Kentucky, and Cincinnati, Ohio," Shaun says. "We feel fortunate to have found this special house in the Garden District, our favorite neighborhood, and we constantly celebrate being 'home.'"

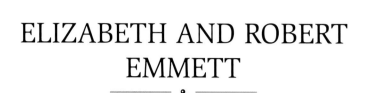

ELIZABETH AND ROBERT EMMETT

Garden District Enchantment

The cotton-candy colored home of Elizabeth and Robert Emmett on First Street in the Garden District was built in the early twentieth century. "Considering that the original owner, who built the house for his son, was the creator of the nectar flavor used in traditional New Orleans snoballs, it makes sense that we have a pink house," Elizabeth says. Snoballs and cotton candy— both indicate a playful approach to living in a grand house with an impressive address.

"With two young boys, we love everything about the house," adds Robert. "We purchased the house in 2010 to accommodate our growing family and immediately embarked on a total renovation to make the home more family friendly, yet preserve and restore the original architectural features of the house."

There is no mistaking that the Emmetts' home is family friendly if you come for a visit during the Christmas holiday season. Walk into the vestibule, and the first room you will find is the sun-filled living room with a large tree, completely laden with lights and ornaments. Stockings are hung on the nearby mantel, which is decorated with greenery and red berry branches.

"Christmas is our favorite holiday," Elizabeth says. "We start decorating immediately after Thanksgiving. It is always a big family event, from selecting the tree to the ritual of adding the decorations." Elizabeth unpacks the tree decorations while listening to Christmas music, and Roberts dresses the tree. Then, sons John-William and Harper choose a small tree for their rooms and get to decorate it as they wish.

"To promote good behavior during the Christmas season,

RIGHT: The Christmas tree shares the holiday spirit in the living room with the fireplace, which is surrounded with red poinsettias. Holiday greens and red berry branches decorate the mantel that holds the Christmas stockings.

OPPOSITE, BOTTOM: A carved lion wearing a Santa cap greets you in the living room.

BELOW: Built in the early-twentieth century, the home was purchased in 2010 and completely remodeled by Elizabeth and Robert Emmett under the guidance of architect Brian Gille.

the 'Elf on the Shelf' makes an appearance immediately after Thanksgiving," she continues. "If the boys are good all day, the next morning the elf leaves them a little present in the pocket on their Advent calendar. Then, there's the tradition of the boys getting together with the neighbor's children to make gingerbread houses, and my mother has a 'cookie day,' where she bakes Christmas cookies with the boys so Santa Claus will have something to eat on Christmas Eve."

Interior designer Curtis Herring, who helped the couple create the comfortable interiors, assisted with the holiday decorating to make everything picture perfect for the Preservation Resource Center's Thirty-Eighth Annual Holiday Home Tour. "We both like the British Colonial/West Indies style after traveling throughout the Caribbean," Elizabeth says. "We inherited the contents of three separate houses full of antiques from around the world, and Curtis did a great

job helping us bring the sometimes-disparate pieces together to create the style we wanted."

Architect Brian Gille was called in to do the renovation and make sure the architectural integrity of the house was preserved while, at the same time, making the house livable for a modern family. "We love coming into our house and knowing we helped preserve it for another generation," Robert says. "We were very fortunate that previous owners had retained the important architectural features such as the pocket doors, fireplaces, molding, and windows."

The Emmetts' home is indeed a joyful place during the holidays. Not only is it a child-friendly setting, but also it is everything the young couple, both attorneys, wanted in a historic home. "We end Christmas Day on a happy note when family members come by for champagne and dessert," Elizabeth says with a smile.

JILL AND ROGER JENKINS

Garden District Enchantment

The Garden District is

full of surprises. Yes, there are the storybook, picture-perfect, colonnaded mansions, yet there also are architectural treasures that you may completely miss if you tour the historic neighborhood in a vehicle. Welcome to the home of Jill and Roger Jenkins, a newer jewel of the historic area that is mostly hidden from the street. Designed by noted architect Paul G. Charbonnet, it was built on Second Street in 1964. "We purchased the house in 2010 because we lived out of state and missed home," Jill says. "Even though career paths have taken us far and wide, we always consider New Orleans home, and we wanted an anchor here."

Enter through the gate and enjoy the manicured gardens and courtyard and you will discover a unique home that was completely redone under the direction of talented residential designer Matthew Voelkel. "Matt did everything," Jill continues. "I gave him free reign and completely trusted him to work his magic."

Christmas is an ideal time to visit the unique home since it features holiday decorations that are in perfect keeping with the contemporary interiors. "Matt was called in the do the decorations," she says. "He hand-selected and custom-ordered each item, then he installed everything."

"I wanted to think outside the box," Matt explains. "My concept was of natural and earthy juxtaposed against metallic and geometrics. I achieved this look by using green moss spheres with illuminated irregular white trees on the

ABOVE: Conical mercury glass trees in a muted metallic color scheme are displayed on the living room coffee table.

TOP RIGHT: The iron gate fronting the sidewalk only gives a hint to the beauty of the garden and home beyond.

BOTTOM RIGHT: Brown cardboard gift boxes are used under the tree to continue the concept of natural and earthy juxtaposed against metallic.

mantle and perfectly round, muted metallic and white ornaments on the large Christmas tree, mixed with conical mercury glass trees in a muted metallic color scheme: silver, white, gray, copper, and gold on the coffee table."

Christmas always means a happy family reunion for the Jenkinses. "Our entire family flies in from different locations around the country to be together in New Orleans for the holidays, and I enjoy creating a holiday atmosphere for all of us to enjoy," Jill says. "Traditionally, we kick off the holiday season by hosting Thanksgiving at our home. We utilize the shuttered carport for extra tables and outdoor seating to accommodate our large extended family. After the traditional Thanksgiving meal, the whole crew comes back to watch the Louisiana State University football game over a steaming bowl of turkey gumbo."

The holiday tradition continues by attending mass on Christmas Eve. "We always look forward to walking to Commander's Palace for a festive dinner. Then, on Christmas morning, we exchange gifts beside the roaring fire in the living room. When the presents are opened, we share a typical Southern breakfast, complete with an egg casserole, grits, and biscuits."

Since Jill and Roger both like to cook, the kitchen was designed for two cooks. "I custom-designed the 16-inch-wide by 7-foot-long island of alder wood that is perfect for two cooks, having plenty of prep room. In keeping with the fashionable rest of the house, I selected the countertops— tiny mosaic tiles for the backsplash and 12-by-24-inch tiles for the floor, all of Calacatta gold marble.

"We wanted the renovation of our home to give us comfort and charm," Jill says. "Everything is understated, yet unique and elegant. We feel like we got everything we wished for and much more. It is definitely a cozy home and welcoming place for our extended family for the holidays."

OPPOSITE, TOP: A group of metallic trees surrounded by gold Christmas ornaments decorate the coffee table in the den. Bleached cypress paneling adds interest to the room.

OPPOSITE, BOTTOM: A simple white bowl of Christmas ornaments is part of the holiday decorations.

ABOVE: Illuminated white trees line the living room mantel, with green moss spheres interspersed at the bottom for interest.

BELOW: A pair of small Christmas trees along with three tree-shaped white candles decorate the console, while a large bowl of white and metallic ornaments is placed on the dining room table for interest.

STEPHANIE AND CLAY SPENCER

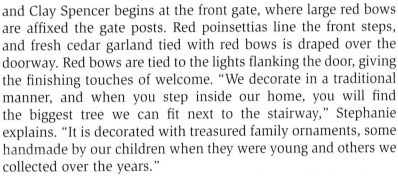

Garden District Enchantment

The spirit of Christmas at the home of Stephanie

OPPOSITE: The grand parlor celebrates the holiday season with a fresh garland with red bows draped on the mantel. Candelabras with red candles flank the large mirror. The elegant silk drapes were done by Gerrie Bremermann of Bremermann Designs.

BELOW: Built in 1895, the Garden District home of Stephanie and Clay Spencer on First Street showcases classic Queen Anne features.

and Clay Spencer begins at the front gate, where large red bows are affixed the gate posts. Red poinsettias line the front steps, and fresh cedar garland tied with red bows is draped over the doorway. Red bows are tied to the lights flanking the door, giving the finishing touches of welcome. "We decorate in a traditional manner, and when you step inside our home, you will find the biggest tree we can fit next to the stairway," Stephanie explains. "It is decorated with treasured family ornaments, some handmade by our children when they were young and others we collected over the years."

Built in 1895, the pristine three-story house displays Queen Anne features, such as a sweeping, curved upper balcony, large front gable, and decorative columns. It is situated on First Street, one of the most fashionable streets in the Garden District.

"This house is special to us because it is where my husband lived as a young man and it was the site of our wedding reception," Stephanie says. "When it came on the market in 2004, we couldn't resist the chance to make it our family home."

Once they owned the house, they immediately began a six-year renovation and restoration of the property, taking care to address special features such as the dentil molding around the cornice, the carved brackets with finials that support the eaves, and the shingled front gable that gives the house its timeless look. The restoration was awarded Best of the 2010 Preservation Award by the Garden District Association. Everything inside was renewed in a traditional style, including four baths, a powder room, and the kitchen breakfast room.

The front parlor is a study in traditional grandeur, with elegant silk drapes, a marble fireplace with a large pier mirror, and antique furnishings, all serving as the backdrop for traditional Christmas decorations, which includes a pair of antique

candelabras on the mantel topped with fresh greens and red bows that fall to the floor. Keepsake stockings hang from the mantel, and angels are displayed on the coffee table. For a light-hearted touch, a Santa pillow embellished with the words "HO, HO, HO" rests on the sofa.

The Christmas tree has a traditional place next to the stairway. The walls in the main reception hall and staircase are covered in an intricate hand-painted design by local artist Jan Drew. Simple crayon drawings by the Spencers' now-grown children, Virginia, Clay IV, and Jared, along with other sentimental ornaments such as family photos in tiny silver frames, adorn the tree.

The library was decorated in a traditional manner by interior designer Gerrie Bremermann of Bremermann Designs. Fresh red roses and greenery, along with red candles, decorate the mantel, while small ornaments are placed in the center of the display.

The dining room table is set with a sterling silver punch bowl and cups ready to share eggnog at the family's open house. It's a festive occasion for the couple to celebrate with their extended family and friends. The red and green theme of the traditional

holiday decorations continues with an arrangement of red roses and red berries, a centerpiece for the large table.

"Christmas is definitely a happy time in our home," Stephanie says. "We have our holiday meal early on Christmas afternoon and enjoy spending time with our family."

OPPOSITE, TOP: The large Christmas tree has its traditional place next to the stairway.

OPPOSITE, BOTTOM: Christmas plates and a small tree decorated with fruit welcome you to the breakfast room.

TOP LEFT: The mantel in the cozy library is decorated with red roses, red berries, and green garland. Red candles in silver candlesticks draped with crystals add the final touch of elegance to the mantel.

TOP RIGHT: A silver punch bowl and cups on the dining room table are ready for the Spencers' annual eggnog party.

BOTTOM RIGHT: A keepsake Nativity scene is placed in front of an arrangement of red roses, red berries, and greens on the antique chest.

CARLI AND FRANK TESSIER

Garden District Enchantment

Two-term mayor of New Orleans Joseph Shakspeare

OPPOSITE: The floor-to-ceiling Christmas tree showcases the special tradition, passed along since Frank was a small child. Frank's parents gave every child in the family a sterling silver Gorham snowflake by Gorham or a Reed and Barton Christmas cross to add to the tree each year. The Tessiers continued the tradition with their three children. Other decorations for the tree are silver balls and ribbon, along with tiny white lights.

BELOW: Built by two-term New Orleans mayor Joseph Shakspeare in 1896, the Camp Street mansion has been owned by the Tessiers since 1989.

and his wife, Antoinette, built a stately mansion on Camp Street in 1896. Unfortunately, Shakspeare never lived in the home; he died just months before it was completed. The house stayed in the Shakspeare family for forty years after it was built. Purchased by Carli and Frank Tessier in 1989, today the neo-classical home is in pristine condition.

"Julie and Banks McClintock, well-known preservationists, have worked tirelessly with us to restore, revitalize, and preserve our historic Garden District home," Carli says. "They carefully researched the original details of the home and returned it to its historically correct roots. It is interesting to note that Julie and Banks were greatly aided by neighbors who had lived on the block for generations and could offer memories and advice. All of the woodwork was restored, a process that took over a year, and we like the fact that the interior of the home showcases the colors and patterns popular in the 1890s."

Christmas is a special time to visit the Tessiers' home. "I always decorate in silver and gold and use only fresh cedar garland and greenery," Carli explains. "Since we have 12½-foot ceilings, I order a special tree in the summer for Christmas. One of our family's traditions which has been passed along since Frank was a small child is the giving of sterling silver snowflakes by Gorham or Christmas crosses by Reed and Barton to every child in the family each year, so our tree represents decades of family Christmas celebrations."

The Tessiers' tree resides majestically in the library adjacent to the monumental nineteenth-century Belle Époque mantel with an arched pediment, centered by a bronze and porcelain clock. The solid marble headpiece is a single block weighing 2,000 pounds and was hydraulically lifted into the house. Frank inherited the 1848 C. Kurtzmann nineteenth-century baby grand piano from his parents.

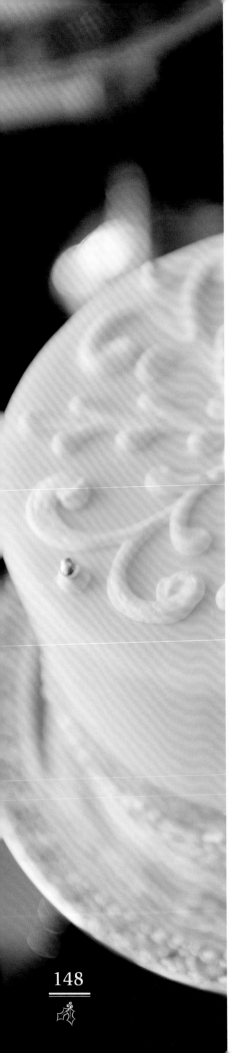

Julie and Banks were called in to help Carli prepare the home for the Preservation Resource Center's Christmas Home Tour. They suggested incorporating mercury glass alongside the traditional silver ornaments. Julie was in charge of decorating the stairway with fresh fruit and artichokes intertwined in layers of fresh cedar garland and gold and silver ribbon.

To add a special touch to the unique decorations, Elizabeth Seaver was called in to arrange all of the flowers, assembling vast amounts of white hydrangeas, white Casablanca lilies, white roses, and bells of Ireland. Carli added white poinsettias and paperwhite narcissus to further enhance the decorations. She also added the final touch of a large gold papier mâché cherub hanging from the unique entrance chandelier from White Oaks, the Duke Mansion in Charlotte, North Carolina.

The dining room is in traditional English taste, with tiger oak wainscoting, cypress woodwork, and a mantel with a crest consisting

TOP LEFT: The holiday table is set with Frank's mother's gold rimmed chargers, Minton china in the Buckingham pattern, Gorham sterling silver flatware in the Chantilly pattern from Carli's great aunt, and a fish set from Frank's great aunt. Waterford crystal and antique table linens, along with an ornate holiday cracker and a gold and silver ornament in the center of each plate, completes the dramatic setting.

TOP RIGHT: The dining room table is dressed for a grand holiday meal. The room is illuminated by a nineteenth-century, eighteen-light bronze and crystal chandelier. A rare eighteenth-century Regence mirror with an intricate gilded carved frame adds interest to the space.

OPPOSITE, LEFT: One of a trio of fodant cakes decorated in snowflakes is displayed atop sterling silver compotes from Frank's mother.

OPPOSITE, RIGHT: The elegant living room is furnished with fine antiques. A circa-1860 Regence round table in the center of the room is prepared for serving fondant cakes from Bittersweet Confections on Magazine Street. The sterling silver compotes holding the cakes are from Frank's mother.

of a crown, three lions, and three *fleurs-de-lis*. The holiday table is set with Frank's mother's gold-rimmed chargers, Minton china in the Buckingham pattern, Gorham's sterling flatware in the Chantilly pattern from Carli's great aunt, and a fish set from Frank's great aunt. Waterford crystal and antique table lines also add to the elegance of the table setting. "I added holiday crackers and placed gold and silver ornaments at every place setting for something extra," Carli says.

"We especially enjoy Christmas when our two children— Dr. Mary Elizabeth McConnell Tessier (and her husband, Joseph Paul Crescenzo III) and Frank Andrew Tessier Jr.— are with us. It is always a joyful occasion to be together."

REGINA AND RONALD "RON" KEEVER

Festive Entertaining

Christmas is a grand meal at the home of Regina and Ronald "Ron" Keever. Make no mistake: both are world travelers and "foodies" in the true sense of the word, not to mention that Regina is co-owner of Bayona Restaurant in the French Quarter with world-class chef Susan Spicer, and that she grew up in a home where food was always a great part of her family's life. (Her childhood home was the grand Elms Mansion on St. Charles Avenue.) "We love it when our children and grandchildren can be home for Christmas and join us for a joyful holiday meal," she says with a smile.

The Keevers' home in Metairie Club Gardens is ideal for entertaining with not only a grand dining room but also the entire back of the home, which features a grand, open floor plan that includes the family room, a sunny breakfast room overlooking the garden, and a state-of-the-art kitchen. "I love it when we are all in the kitchen preparing the meal," she continues. "I love to cook, and for my holiday meal I always incorporate some of Susan's recipes from Bayona. She is such an imaginative chef, and we have had a wonderful relationship working together."

Regina is a collector of recipes, always keeping old favorites such as her Crown Pork Roast with Madeira Stuffing and Sauce that has been the centerpiece of her holiday meal for more than thirty years, and then adding something newer and imaginative such as

ABOVE: The holiday feast has star billing on the buffet.

LEFT: Fine green Steuben art glass dishes and glassware dress the table, while the Grand Baroque sterling flatware and antique Irish linen tablecloth and napkins complete the grandeur of the table setting.

OPPOSITE: The Keevers' elegant dining room in their Metairie Club Gardens home offers an intimate setting for their Christmas meal.

the Roasted Beet and Shaved Fennel Salad. "I always loved to eat the Mile High Ice Cream Pie with Chocolate Sauce at the Pontchartrain," she says. "Now I make my very own version of the recipe using peppermint ice cream. It's a perfect dessert to end any meal."

Louisiana Oyster Toasts

This sumptuous appetizer stars poached oysters in an elegant cream sauce. The oyster mixture is spooned over buttered and toasted brioche triangles and topped with crispy pancetta and chives. The flavors of this dish are delicious with champagne and have a holiday feel, but they are delicious anytime you can get great oysters. You could also toss the warm sauté with bow tie pasta for a decidedly rich Sunday supper.

6 oz. pancetta, diced
¼ cup white wine or vermouth
1 pt. shucked oysters, drained and rinsed
1 tbsp. butter, plus additional, softened, for spreading
¼ cup finely chopped onion
¼ cup finely chopped celery
2-3 leeks (about 1 cup), washed and thinly sliced
¾ cup oyster mushrooms, sliced
2 tbsp. flour
¼ cup milk
½ cup cream
½ tsp. chopped fresh thyme or sage
1 tbsp. fresh lemon juice
Salt and pepper to taste
Hot sauce to taste
4 ½"-thick slices good-quality white bread or brioche, halved diagonally into triangles
Minced scallions or snipped fresh chives, optional, for garnish

In a large skillet, cook the pancetta until crispy. Transfer it to a plate covered in paper towels, then drain the skillet of all but 1 tbsp. fat; set the skillet aside.

Heat the white wine in a medium skillet over medium-high heat. When it starts to simmer, add the oysters and poach just until the edges start to curl, about 4 minutes (reduce the heat if simmer gets too lively). Drain the oysters in a fine colander placed over a large bowl, reserving the poaching liquid.

Reheat the skillet with bacon fat over medium-high heat, and add butter. When foaming subsides, add the onion, celery, and leeks, and cook until fragrant and softened, 3 to 4 minutes. Stir in the mushrooms and cook for 5 minutes more. Sprinkle the vegetables with flour, then whisk in the reserved oyster-poaching liquid. Simmer over medium heat, continuously whisking, for 3 minutes. Add the milk, cream, and thyme, and bring to a boil. Reduce the heat and simmer gently until thickened and creamy, about 5 minutes. Add the lemon juice and salt, pepper, and hot sauce to taste.

When the sauce is thick enough to coat the back of a spoon, remove it from the heat and keep warm. Toast the bread, spread with softened butter, and place on individual plates. Stir the oysters into the cream sauce over low heat, and warm through. To serve, spoon the oysters and sauce over the toast and sprinkle with pancetta. Top with scallions or chives, if desired. **Serves 4**

Roasted Beet and Shaved Fennel Salad

This colorful salad that is sometimes featured at Bayona restaurant offers an irresistible combination of flavors.

3 beets
2 fennel bulbs
5 oz. arugula
1 small sweet onion, chopped, optional
Balsamic reduction
4 oz. crumbled Feta cheese

Preheat oven to 375 degrees.

Wash and dry the beets. Roast whole, with skin, in a pan with 1 cup of water for about 1½ hours or until tender. Once beets are cool, peel them and cut in quarters.

Shave fennel using a mandolin slicer to make about 2 to 3 cups. Toss arugula with fennel, onion (if using), and balsamic reduction; divide between four plates. Top with Feta cheese and roasted beets. Serve immediately. **Serves 4**

Balsamic Reduction: Reduce balsamic vinegar to about ¼ cup in sauté pan (approximately 7 minutes). Pour in a bowl and whisk in olive oil in a slow, steady stream. Season with salt and pepper to taste.

Recipe courtesy Susan Spicer

½-¾ cup balsamic vinegar
½ cup olive oil
Salt and pepper to taste

Crown Pork Roast with Madeira Stuffing and Sauce

This elegant main course has been the centerpiece of Regina's holiday meal for more than thirty years, and it never ceases to delight her family and friends.

Preheat oven to 375 degrees.

Lay pork chop flat, fat-side down, and slice a third of the way through each chop for ease of serving. Stand roast up and tie ends together, forming a circle. (Your butcher also can help prepare the roast by frenching and slicing the pork in advance.)

Make the marinade by whisking honey, barbecue sauce, and Madeira wine together. Brush pork roast with marinade. Save remaining marinade for sauce.

In a large bowl, combine crackers, dry mustard, and brown sugar. Sauté celery, onion, and green pepper in butter until soft, about 8 to 10 minutes. Add mushrooms and sauté for 5 minutes more. Add vegetables to cracker mixture. Stir in sage, vinegar, parsley, eggs, Madeira wine, salt and pepper to taste, and bacon.

Roast the pork for 1½ to 2 hours, or until the temperature of the meat reaches 165 degrees. If needed, cover roast with foil to avoid becoming too dark. Bake stuffing for 30 to 40 minutes. Add remaining marinade to drippings in roasting pan. Reduce in a saucepan until slightly thickened, and serve alongside meat.

Present roast filled with the stuffing in the crown. Your butcher can supply paper for the frenched bones—it makes for a festive presentation. **Serves 8-12**

16-rib crown pork roast, rib bones frenched

Marinade
¾ cup honey
¾ cup homemade or favorite barbeque sauce
½ cup Madeira wine

Stuffing
3 cups crushed Ritz crackers
1½ tbsp. dry mustard
2 tbsp. brown sugar
½ cup chopped celery
1 cup chopped onion
1 cup chopped green pepper
½ stick butter
1 cup finely chopped mushrooms
1 tsp. sage
1 tbsp. vinegar
½ cup chopped parsley
2 eggs, beaten
½ cup Madeira wine
Salt and pepper to taste
1 cup chopped, crisp apple-smoked bacon, or 2 cups finely chopped ham

3 sticks butter
4-5 medium yams, chopped
1 cup sugar
1 cup brown sugar
2 sticks of cinnamon
1 tsp. vanilla
½ tsp. mace
1 unpeeled orange, sliced and seeded
1 unpeeled lemon, sliced and seeded
1 cup water or orange juice
4 large navel oranges, halved
Large marshmallows

Candied Yams
in Orange Cups

This delightful holiday side was always served by Regina's mother, Josie, and Regina has continued to include it as part of her Christmas tradition.

Heat butter until melted in a small pot, and add all ingredients through water. Stir and bring to a strong boil over high heat for 10 minutes. Stir, reduce heat, and simmer, covered, for 20 minutes until yams are tender, stirring occasionally. Cool; remove cinnamon and citrus. Purée yams.

If you like, reduce the remaining liquid from the yam pot until syrupy.

Remove all pulp from the navel oranges. Fill with yam purée. To serve, top filled oranges with marshmallows and broil for 2 minutes. Drizzle with extra syrup from the yams. **Serves 8**

3 tbsp. butter, olive oil, or rendered bacon or duck fat
1 medium onion and 1 smoked onion*, chopped
2 tbsp. garlic, minced
12-15 cups greens (a mixture of mustards, turnips, or collards is best, but you can add red chard, beet tops, kale, or other hearty greens if you need), stemmed, washed, and chopped
2 tsp. cider vinegar
Salt, pepper, and hot sauce to taste

Smothered Greens
with Smoked Onions

Bayona restaurant prepares a variety of greens to accompany many entrées. Because of the Southern fell, this is one of Regina's favorites.

Melt butter or oil in a wide, thick-bottomed pan. Heat oil and sauté onion for about 5 minutes, without coloring. Add garlic and cook 2 more minutes. Stir in greens and cook over medium-high heat until wilted, about 5 minutes. Cover pan and cook for 10 to 15 more minutes, then remove lid and turn heat up to evaporate some of the liquid in the pot. Taste for bitterness; if still bitter, reduce heat and cook a little

longer. When greens are flavorful but not biting, sprinkle in vinegar and season to taste with salt, pepper, and hot sauce. Keep warm until ready to serve. **Serves 12**

*To smoke onions: Cut in half and place on a grill or home-style smoker. Cover with dome and smoke for about 20 to 30 minutes. Keep refrigerated in plastic bags or sealed containers for at least a week.

Mile High Ice Cream Pie with Chocolate Sauce

Mile High Pie was made famous by the Pontchartrain Hotel, located on St. Charles Avenue in New Orleans. Regina continues to delight her holiday guests with her own version of this presentation.

In the pie crust, layer chocolate ice cream (first), vanilla (second), and peppermint (third) in a dome shape. Freeze in between each layer. To help build layers, cut ice cream gallons in half lengthwise before placing in the pie crust. Freeze as soon as possible.

Beat egg whites with vanilla and cream of tartar until soft peaks form. Slowly add sugar until stiff and glossy. Cover frozen pie completely with egg whites.

Place under an oven broiler for a few moments, being careful not to burn. Freeze until ready to serve.

When ready to enjoy, generously serve chocolate sauce over each slice of pie.

Chocolate Sauce: Place half the heavy cream (⅜ cup), both chocolates, and sugar in a double boiler until sugar is dissolved and chocolate is melted, smooth, and thick. Add remaining cream as needed to achieve pouring consistency.

1 baked 9" pie crust
½ gallon each vanilla, chocolate, and peppermint ice cream, slightly softened
8 egg whites
½ tsp. vanilla
¼ tsp. cream of tartar
½ cup sugar

¾ cup heavy cream, divided
6 oz. German sweet chocolate
6 oz. semisweet chocolate
1½ cups sugar

LINDA AND PETER TUFTON

Festive Entertaining

There was a time when grand entertaining in

OPPOSITE: The dining room in the Tuftons' Garden District home provides a picture-perfect setting for a grand Christmas meal.

BELOW: Antique Spode plates from Tiffany's rest on silver chargers. The sterling flatware was inherited from Peter's family. Baccarat 'Capri' crystal completes the setting.

Garden District homes was a part of daily life, but it isn't as common today due to busy schedules and a myriad of great restaurants, where dining with family or guests is effortless. Then, there are couples such as Linda and Dr. Peter Tufton, who still enjoy sitting down to a fine meal in their elegantly appointed dining room on a quiet Garden District street.

"There is something special about sharing a meal at home with friends and family," explains Peter, a dentist, who does most of the cooking at home. "We especially enjoy entertaining in our home around the holiday season, very much like my parents and grandparents did in their day." Fortunately, much of what the Tuftons use today for hosting was inherited, such as the Kirk Repousse sterling flatware that came from Peter's mother and father, Anita and Peter Tufton. "It was from the wedding of my parents, so it has sentimental value to our family." The cut glass water pitcher, linen napkins, and fish service are from Peter's mother's parents, Camilla and Michael Pons, and the stag horn salad servers from Peter's paternal grandparents, Mary and Francis Tufton.

"After opening our presents on Christmas morning, we attend Mass and return to our home," Linda says. "The final preparations for our meal start. When all is done, we go into the dining room and begin our meal. Each year, a different member of the family says Grace. We take our time to enjoy each course and each other. We talk about family members who are no longer with us and past Christmases. We look to the future when we will need more space at the table and more stories to tell."

The Tuftons' five children—Margaret, Michael, Anne, Ashley, and Meredith—were brought up enjoying the holiday grandeur, and although there is a friendly casualness when the house is filled with their friends, there is never a complaint when the holidays come around and a Christmas meal is enjoyed in a grand manor.

Peter shares his family's favorite recipes for your enjoyment.

Poached Salmon

The salmon is a nice way to start a meal. A healthy dish, it is served cold and can be prepared in advance—an important attribute for a Christmas feast.

2 lbs. salmon fillets
1 750 ml bottle Riesling wine
1 bunch fresh dill
2 shallots, chopped
1 tsp. salt
½ tsp. white pepper

Place salmon fillets in a wide-rimmed sauce pan. Cover the salmon with wine. Place the chopped shallots and sprigs of fresh dill in the poaching liquid. Heat liquid until just before boiling. Cook for 8 minutes or until salmon is opaque. Serve with dill sauce. Maybe served hot or cold. **Serves 6**

1½ cups sour cream
Juice of 1 lemon
1½ tbsp. horseradish
3 tbsp. fresh dill, chopped
2 tbsp. fresh chives, chopped

Dill Sauce: Combine all ingredients in a small bowl.

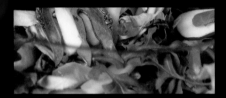

Endive Salad

This salad is light, and the pepper flavor of the watercress and arugula stimulates your appetite for the next course.

2 Belgian endives, cut into strips
1 bunch radishes, diced
4 cups baby arugula
1 bunch watercress, stems removed

Mix all ingredients together, then add dressing. **Serves 6**

½ cup olive oil
2 tbsp. black truffle oil
½ cup red wine vinegar
½ tsp. salt
½ tsp. black pepper

Dressing: Whisk together all ingredients in a small bowl.

Italian Chicken Roll

This recipe comes from Peter's father, which he developed over time and would make on special occasions. He liked to show off how fast he could debone a chicken. Peter once asked him if he would make the recipe for a party of fifty. He did, but then it became Peter's job from then on to make the dish.

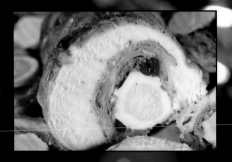

1 3-lb. chicken, deboned
Salt and pepper to taste
3 oz. ham, sliced
3 oz. Mortadella sausage
3 oz. Genoa salami
½ cup breadcrumbs
½ cup black Kalamata olives, chopped
5 hard-boiled eggs, ends removed
   to form a log

Preheat oven 375 degrees.
   Place deboned chicken, skin-side down and head facing you, on a clean work surface. Sprinkle chicken with salt and pepper. Place the ham on the chicken, followed by the Mortadella and salami, leaving 1″ of chicken as a border. Sprinkle with breadcrumbs, then chopped olives. Place the hard-boiled eggs close to the end and roll up the chicken. Tie with string to secure, and roast for 40 minutes or until golden brown.
   Let stand for 15 minutes, then slice into ½″-thick slices. May be served hot or cold. **Serves 6**

Golden Potatoes

The golden potatoes are a recipe from Linda's aunt Pat Koscelnick. It is a must-have dish for every holiday dinner. The Tuftons have tried other potato recipes, but they always return to this dish.

Place potatoes, skins on, in a pot of water with the garlic. Cook until fork tender. Drain, and chill until cold. Peel and grate the potatoes, then transfer into a large mixing bowl.

Preheat oven to 325 degrees.

Melt butter and cheese together in a small skillet over low heat. Remove from heat and blend in sour cream, onion, salt, and pepper. Add hot sauce to taste. Pour over potatoes and mix gently.

Transfer into shallow, buttered baking dish. Bake for 30 minutes. **Serves 6**

6 medium potatoes
6 cloves garlic, peeled
¼ cup butter
2 cups grated cheddar cheese
1 pt. sour cream
½ cup chopped green onion
1 tsp. salt
½ tsp. pepper
Hot sauce to taste

Spinach-Stuffed Tomatoes

Peter likes to have items that look attractive on the plate, so color is important. The red tomatoes and green stuffing are perfect for Christmas.

Preheat oven to 350 degrees.

Melt butter in a saucepan over low heat. Add flour, stirring constantly; do not let flour brown. Add heavy cream and Boursin. When sauce is smooth, add the spinach.

Cut tomatoes in half, and scoop out the insides, being careful not to pierce the skin. Spoon spinach mixture into tomatoes. Bake for 10 minutes. **Serves 8**

2 tbsp. butter
2 tbsp. flour
1 cup heavy cream
5.2 oz. Boursin garlic and fine herb cheese
10 oz. frozen, chopped spinach, thawed and squeezed dry
4 medium-sized tomatoes

Berry Trifle

Cut pound cake into 1" slices and spread with strawberry preserves. Place a layer of cake, preserve-side up, in the bottom of a trifle bowl. Top with some of the blueberries, strawberries, and brandy cream. Repeat layers, ending with cake only.

Top with whipped cream and remaining berries.

1 vanilla pound cake
1 cup strawberry preserves
1 pt. blueberries
2 pt. strawberries
Brandy cream
Whipped cream, for serving

Brandy Cream: Heat half-and-half in a stainless-steel saucepan until almost boiling.

Meanwhile, beat the egg yolks and sugar on medium speed in an electric mixer, fitted with paddle attachment, until thick. Reduce speed to low and add cornstarch. Beat on medium-low until combined. Pour hot half-and-half into egg mixture. Return mixture to the saucepan and heat until thick, about 7 minutes. Stir in vanilla and brandy. Strain to remove any lumps, if necessary.

Refrigerate until cold. **Serves 6**

3 cups half-and-half
12 large egg yolks
1 cup sugar
4 tbsp. sifted cornstarch
1 tsp. vanilla
1 tbsp. brandy

MARY AND ROLAND VON KURNATOWSKI

Festive Entertaining

Mary and Roland von Kurnatowski thought it would

OPPOSITE: The two-story covered courtyard in the center of the home features a Christmas tree, while the second-story balcony that overlooks the space is festooned with lighted garland.

BELOW: To complete the party menu, a Popeyes station is strategically located in the courtyard.

be a perfect home for entertaining when they first saw the interesting 8,000-square-foot structure on St. Charles Avenue near Gallier Hall, built in 1840. "We envisioned open spaces, unobstructed by too much furniture, where we could have a comfortable home, yet with plenty of room to entertain our friends or to open our home to worthy causes," says Mary, a talented designer who spends most of her time working with non-profit organizations, such as the Tipitina's Foundation, a unique program that supports the irreplaceable music community and culture of Louisiana and New Orleans in many ways, including having provided millions of dollars' worth of musical instruments to Louisiana schools. Roland owns Tipitina's, so it's a perfect harmony for the couple.

The couple's annual holiday party has become a noted event to close the holiday season, since it is staged on New Year's Eve. While a catering firm is called in to do some of the food preparation, Mary is the star of the dessert table, which takes over the dining room for the event. "I love baking, and everybody expects a slice of my Italian Cream Cake frosted with coconut or one of my Red Velvet Cupcakes," she says. "I also have two other special dessert treats that are popular: Unforgettable Forget Me Meringues and Chocolate Nests." Just in case your sweet tooth has not been satisfied, Mary also spreads a treasure hunt of candy on the mirrored chest in the front parlor.

The buffet features such local favorites as gumbo and black-eyed peas, dishes that Mary always prepares. Pigeon Catering makes the Celebration Salad of mixed greens blended with walnuts, sun-dried tomatoes, golden raisins, and blue cheese and tossed with a pepper jelly vinaigrette; a roasted pork loin stuffed with smoked boudin and wrapped with Applewood bacon; and Gouda Mashed Potatoes. For *lagniappe*, Mary saves a special spot in the courtyard for a station of Popeyes fried chicken and biscuits.

It all adds up to the perfect party to end the holiday season.

TOP: The dining room is devoted a special dessert table, with treats prepared by Mary.

BOTTOM: The top of the mirrored chest in the front parlor is reserved for candy treats.

Italian Cream Cake
with Coconut Frosting

Preheat oven to 325 degrees. Grease 3 9" cake pans, and line the bottoms with wax paper.

Cream the butter with shortening and sugar in a medium bowl. Add egg yolks, one at a time, and vanilla, followed by baking soda and buttermilk.

Combine flour with the buttermilk mixture in fourths, ending with the buttermilk. Add coconut and chopped pecans to the batter.

Beat the egg whites until stiff peaks form, then fold into the cake batter.

Gently pour batter into cake pans, and bake for 35 minutes until cake begins to loosen from the edges of the pan. Cool layers thoroughly before filling and icing.

To make the icing, blend together cream cheese, butter, vanilla, and confectioners' sugar. Spread between the layers, building into a three-layer cake. Spread remaining icing on the top and sides of the cake. Add coconut on top of the icing, and top with fresh roses just before serving. If you wish, sprinkle a little more coconut on top of roses—it almost looks like snow!

Serves 20

1 stick butter
½ cup shortening
2 cups sugar
5 large eggs, separated
1 tsp. vanilla
1 tsp. baking soda
1 cup buttermilk
2 cups plain flour
½ cup shredded coconut
1 cup chopped pecans

Icing
1 cup cream cheese
1 stick butter
1 tsp. vanilla
1 lb. confectioners' sugar
½ cup shredded coconut

Unforgettable Forget Me Meringues

Mary does not recommend making them *too* far ahead of time, or they may be gone before the guests arrive! These sit overnight in the oven, so be sure to sneak one (or two) for yourself for breakfast.

8 large egg whites
3 cups granulated sugar
1 cup Heath chocolate-covered toffee bits
1 cup pecans, finely chopped and toasted

Preheat oven to 350 degrees. Line 4 baking sheets with parchment paper.

In a large, chilled, stainless-steel bowl, beat egg whites and sugar at high speed with an electric mixer until soft peaks form and the sugar is completely dissolved. Using a spatula, gently fold in Heath toffee and chopped pecans by hand.

Drop meringues by rounded teaspoonfuls onto the prepared baking sheets. Place in the preheated oven, and then turn the oven off. Let meringues stand in oven for 10 hours or overnight. Do not open the oven, not even once. No peeking!

These can be made a couple of days ahead of time and then stored in tightly sealed containers. **Serves 24**

Red Velvet Cupcakes

1 15.25-oz. box white cake mix
2 tbsp. cocoa powder
1 3.4-oz. box instant vanilla pudding
2 oz. red food coloring

Frosting
1 cup milk
¼ cup flour
Dash of salt
½ cup shortening
1 cup sugar
1 stick butter
2 tsp. vanilla

Preheat oven to 350 degrees. Place 24 foil cupcake liners in a cupcake pan

In a medium bowl, combine cake mix, cocoa powder, and vanilla pudding. Add the red food coloring to a measuring cup, and fill with water to reach 1 cup (or quantity indicated on cake mix box), and mix as usual into the pudding mixture. Pour into cupcake pans and bake for 12 to 14 minutes, until a toothpick inserted in the center pulls out clean. Let cupcakes cool thoroughly before icing, 2 to 3 hours or overnight.

To make the frosting, combine milk, flour, and salt over a low flame, stirring constantly so it won't lump, until it has the consistency of pudding. Let cool.

Cream shortening, sugar, butter, and vanilla (or coconut, if you prefer). Add cooled milk mixture to shortening mixture, and beat until smooth. Keep in the refrigerator until ready to use.

When ready to serve, top each cupcake with frosting. **Serves 24**

Chocolate Nests

These treats are tasty and really easy to make. They are good for making ahead and storing, especially if you have a lot of self-control. These look good with either white chocolate or milk chocolate—they are so cute!

Preheat oven to 300 degrees. Line a baking sheet with wax paper.

Empty the sweetened coconut onto an ungreased half-pan baking sheet, and spread it out with a couple of forks. Toast the coconut, watching carefully so it doesn't burn. Coconut will start to toast around the edges first. Every few minutes, stir the coconut so it toasts evenly.

Place a large stainless-steel bowl inside a large skillet that has about an inch of water over low heat. Make certain that no water winds up in the stainless steel bowl, or it will ruin the chocolate. Add chocolate to the bowl, and stir gently. Once the chocolate is completely melted, stir in the toasted coconut. If you're feeling adventurous, add in finely chopped dried apricots or other dried fruit, almonds, or sunflower seeds, a little at a time, making certain that any additions are completely covered with chocolate. .

Drop rounded teaspoonfuls of the mixture onto the lined baking sheet, and then refrigerate till the nests harden, about 10 minutes.
Serves 30

7 oz. sweetened coconut
20 oz. white or milk chocolate bark, chopped into pieces
Finely chopped dried apricots or other dried fruit, toasted slivered almonds, or toasted sunflower seeds, optional

KIT AND BILLY WOHL

Festive Entertaining

Kit and Billy Wohl's home and

RIGHT: The feast is displayed on a round table in a unique holiday setting.

BELOW: The grand setting for the Wohls' holiday meal captures the excitement of Christmas. The Venetian chandelier was dressed by Leslie Massony and Monique Chauvin of Mitch's Flowers.

studio is reminiscent of an Italian palazzo. "Perhaps only in New Orleans would you find an elegant Palladian-style penthouse," wrote Carol Flake Chapman for a *House and Garden* magazine feature on the Wohls' art-filled space.

It's a hidden gem where galas have been staged and holidays have been welcomed with a gusto only found in New Orleans, even though Kit's passion for writing and photography has translated into eleven cookbooks, keeping her too busy to frequently entertain at home. "I love everything about entertaining at home," she says as she sits in the grand salon of their home. "Cooking is an art and a form of creative expression. Food is distinctive in form, color, texture, and flavor. The selection, preparation, and presentation of a meal are as creative as any art project. Best of all, it nurtures both the body and spirit."

The Wohls' large dream kitchen is perfectly suited for test cooking or preparing a grand meal. "I included oysters, which Billy and I love," she explains as she describes her holiday menu. "Oysters are a celebration on the half shell—no event is complete without them—and it was a joy to write and photograph the *P&J Oyster Cookbook* (Pelican Publishing Company) with the Sunseri family. Then, when I discovered Leslie Massony's handmade oyster plates, it seemed only natural to feature them as the star of the artful table setting." Each plate is an original by Leslie

and Monique Chauvin, who owns Mitch's Flowers. They founded Oysteria, Inc., to produce and market their plates in 2010.

Kit makes no apologies for offering both raw oysters and Oysters Rockefeller on the same menu. "It's just the way we entertain in New Orleans," she adds with a smile.

RIGHT: Celebrations in New Orleans are highlighted by oyster dressings—everyone has a family favorite.

Oysters Rockefeller

Oyster aficionados have long experimented by trying to replicate Antoine's original Oysters Rockefeller, which the restaurant promises has no spinach. We do add spinach because it works for us. There's no better reason.

1 bunch green onions
1 celery heart
1 lb. frozen spinach, thawed and squeezed dry
¼ cup flat-leaf parsley, leaves only
2 sticks butter, melted
2 tbsp. anchovy paste
Juice of 1 lemon
4 tbsp. Worcestershire sauce
4 oz. Herbsaint or Pernod
½ cup seasoned breadcrumbs, divided
Hot sauce to taste
Salt and freshly ground black pepper to taste
1 qt. shucked oysters, or 18 to 24 oysters on the half-shell

Preheat oven to 375 degrees.

Cut the green onions and celery into ½" pieces. Place in a food processor with the spinach and parsley; process until finely chopped. Add the melted butter, anchovy paste, lemon juice, and Worcestershire sauce, and process until smooth.

Empty the food processor into a 1½-quart saucepan, and add the Herbsaint or Pernod and half (¼ cup) of the breadcrumbs. Simmer over medium heat for 5 minutes.

Add hot sauce, salt, and pepper to taste.

Place shucked oysters in a casserole dish so they cover the bottom, or oysters on the half shell in a baking dish filled with rock salt. Top the oysters with the Rockefeller sauce, and sprinkle lightly with the remaining half (¼ cup) of the breadcrumbs. Bake until brown and bubbly on top, about 20 minutes. Let sit briefly; serve hot. **Serves 4-6**

Seafood Gumbo

It's hardly a celebration without gumbo, and this recipe is a favorite of Kit's. Gumbo is one of New Orleans's most versatile—and famous—soups, making use of whatever proteins are on hand. A small portion can serve as a starter; larger ones make a full meal. Poppy Tooker, an accomplished gumbo throw-down champion, helped to refine this recipe.

1 cup plus 2 tbsp. cooking oil, divided
2 lbs. okra, sliced ¼" thick
1½ cups flour
2 onions, chopped
1 bell pepper, chopped
2 stalks celery, chopped
6 gumbo crabs
6 fresh tomatoes, peeled and crushed
1 clove garlic
2 tbsp. thyme
1 bay leaf
½ gallon shrimp or seafood stock
Salt and freshly ground black pepper to taste
1 pt. raw oysters
5 lbs. shrimp, peeled and boiled
1 bunch green onions, chopped
6 to 10 cups cooked rice, for serving

Heat 2 tbsp. of the cooking oil in a large pan over medium-high heat. Fry the sliced okra until lightly browned; drain and set aside.

In a large Dutch oven or stock pot over medium heat, heat the remaining 1 cup of oil, and gradually whisk in the flour. Make a roux by continually stirring the flour and oil until they are completely combined. Continue stirring until the roux reaches a light brown color. Add the onion, and stir until the roux has reached a darker, chocolate brown color. Add the celery and bell pepper. Sauté for 5 minutes, then add the gumbo crabs, tomatoes, okra, garlic, thyme, bay leaf, and shrimp stock. Season with salt and pepper to taste. Let simmer for at least 45 minutes.

Add the oysters, shrimp, and green onions 10 minutes before serving. Serve warm in a shallow bowl over cooked rice. **Serves 10-12**

Roasted Goose

After a Thanksgiving turkey, roasted goose adds festive flavor to the traditional holiday meal—and cooks much faster. A bonus is the resulting goose fat, ideal to save for use in future recipes. A dressing of apples and cabbage is a savory salute.

The night before you plan to roast the goose, remove the contents from the cavity and discard. Trim and discard any loose skin around the neck. Rub the goose generously with Kosher salt. Place the goose in a large bowl or deep pan, and cover with salt water. Loosely cover with plastic wrap, and refrigerate overnight.

The day of, remove the goose from the bowl and let sit at room temperature for 30 to 60 minutes. Preheat the oven to 425 degrees.

Using paper towels, dry the goose inside and out. Season generously with salt and pepper inside and out. With a fork, pierce the goose all over. Place the goose on a roasting pan, breast-side down, and place in the oven for 30 minutes.

Remove the pan from the oven, and transfer the drippings to a medium-sized heatproof bowl with a ladle or large spoon. Flip the goose breast side up, baste with the drippings, and return to the oven for another 30 minutes.

Remove goose from the oven again, and reduce heat to 350 degrees. Transfer any drippings out of the pan and return the goose to the oven. Basting and removing drippings as needed, cook until a meat probe inserted into the thickest part of the thigh registers 165 degrees. If the bird begins to brown too quickly, cover loosely with tinfoil.

Once roasted, transfer the bird to a cutting board, and let rest for at least 30 minutes. Set the roasting pan aside. Make the stuffing.

To serve, place the goose on a platter and surround with stuffing. **Serves 6**

Goose Stuffing: Toss the apple cubes in lemon juice.

In a large sauté pan, heat the goose fat over medium heat and sauté the apple cubes until lightly browned. Add the onions and continue to cook until onions are transparent. Add the cabbage and cook until just softened.

1 7-9 lb. goose, thawed if frozen
Kosher salt to taste
Freshly ground black pepper to taste

2 green apples, cubed into 1" pieces
1 tbsp. lemon juice
3 tbsp. goose fat
1 large white onion, chopped
1 red cabbage, shredded

Brussels Sprouts and Pomegranate Salad

Thinly shaved Brussels sprouts take the place of more traditional greens for a refreshing salad. The splash of red pomegranate seeds adds holiday cheer.

Remove the core and dark outer leaves from the Brussels sprouts. Peel the remaining leaves into a large bowl of cold water and soak for 5 minutes. Drain thoroughly.

Vigorously whisk the olive oil and lemon juice together until emulsified. Season with salt.

In a large serving bowl, toss the Brussels sprouts, pomegranate seeds, and vinaigrette. Serve immediately. **Serves 6**

2 lbs. fresh Brussels sprouts
½ cup extra-virgin olive oil
Juice of 2 lemons
2 tsp. salt
½ cup fresh pomegranate seeds

Figgy Bread Pudding Flambé

This recipe takes the city's abundance of figs and passion for bread pudding and puts these stars in alliance to be flambéed in a ceremonial finale of a magnificent repast.

In a medium-sized bowl, soak the dried figs in the brandy for several hours or overnight.

Preheat oven to 150 degrees.

In a large bowl, break the French bread into pieces. Break the eggs over the bread pieces and mix well. Add the sugar, vanilla, and pecans.

Reserving the brandy, drain the figs, and add them to the bread mixture. Add the milk, one cup at a time, until the bread is moist enough that milk runs through your fingers when squeezed.

Spoon the mixture into a buttered 8" x 12" baking pan and bake for 40 minutes. Remove from oven and let sit for 10 minutes.

Meanwhile, in a small saucepan, heat the preserved figs in their liquid and simmer until the liquid has reduced by half. Add the reserved brandy and flambé. Serve over the figgy pudding. **Serves 6**

1 cup dried figs, quartered
1 cup brandy
1 loaf stale French bread
8 eggs
1 cup sugar
1 tbsp. vanilla extract
1 cup pecans, chopped
3-4 cups milk
1 10-oz. jar preserved figs

ANTOINE'S RESTAURANT

Holiday Eats

Dining at the venerable Antoine's Restaurant at

OPPOSITE: **A large Christmas tree has a place of honor in a corner of the main dining room at Antoine's.**

BELOW: **Réveillon dinner at Antoine's.**

713 St. Louis Street in the French Quarter is a memorable experience. Opened in 1840, Antoine's has the distinction of being the oldest continuously operating restaurant in New Orleans. It is even more noteworthy that the same family has always run the iconic establishment.

Each December, Antoine's is a fairyland of Christmas with a large Christmas tree filling a corner of the large center dining room on the first floor and holiday decorations greeting you in each of the restaurant's fourteen dining rooms. One of the largest dining establishments in New Orleans, seven hundred diners can be accommodated at one time. It is an ideal place to experience the traditional réveillon menu, with four courses of local favorites offered at a set price.

Noted for its French-Creole cuisine, the fixed-price meal includes specialties prepared by Chef Michael Regua, such as Louisiana Shrimp au Gratin, Noël Salad, and Chicken Rochambeau, a dish that offers delightful layers of a slice of ham, Rochambeau sauce, sautéed chicken breast, and Béarnaise sauce, made famous by Antoine's. Then, to end the meal, there is a delightful Eggnog Bread Pudding with Praline Rum Sauce.

Nothing about Antoine's is ordinary. Here, dining in a grand manner is still an honored institution, and professional waiters pride themselves in offering noteworthy service. The building itself is full of legends as well, including private dining rooms that have names connected to New Orleans Carnival, such as Rex, Proteus, and Twelfth Night.

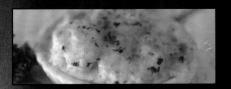

5 oz. shredded Monterey and cheddar cheese, divided
1 oz. breadcrumbs
6 oz. fresh Louisiana shrimp, peeled and deveined
1 tbsp. butter
1 cup Béchamel sauce
Salt and white pepper to taste

½ cup butter
½ cup all-purpose flour
7 oz. half-and-half

1 bunch watercress
1 small head iceberg lettuce
1 small head romaine lettuce
1 small head escarole
20 red grapes
2 oz. shaved carrots
3 oz. dried cranberries
3 oz. chopped walnuts
4 oz. feta cheese
Strawberry vinaigrette

5 oz. olive oil
3 oz. white vinegar
Pinch salt and white pepper
½ oz. dry mustard
1 oz. sugar
8-10 strawberries, cut in half

Louisiana Shrimp au Gratin

Preheat oven to 375 degrees.

Blend 3 oz. of the cheese and breadcrumbs, and set aside. Sauté the shrimp in the butter till ¾ of the way cooked (pink and slightly firm), add Béchamel sauce and the rest of the cheese, and simmer until the shrimp are fully cooked. Add salt and pepper to taste. Put in 4 4-oz. baking dishes or ramekins, top with rest of the mixed cheese. Brown in the oven and serve. **Serves 4**

Béchamel Sauce: Blend butter and flour together over medium heat, but don't brown. Add half-and-half, and cook until thickened.

Noël Salad

Break greens into 1″ pieces, wash in cold ice water, and mix together.

Divide the greens on 4 plates, then top with the grapes, carrots, cranberries, walnuts, and feta, evenly divided between the plates. Drizzle with strawberry vinaigrette. **Serves 4**

Strawberry Vinaigrette: Place all ingredients in a blender. Blend until smooth. Shake well before using.

Chicken Rochambeau

Season chicken with salt and pepper to taste. Sauté until browned and fully cooked; set aside.

Place 1 slice of ham each on 4 plates. Top with Rochambeau Sauce, followed by chicken breasts. Top with Béarnaise sauce. **Serves 4**

Rochambeau Sauce: Sauté onion in butter until lightly brown; add flour, and cook for 1 to 2 minutes. Add sugar, white vinegar, brown chicken stock, and salt and pepper to taste. Simmer over medium heat until sauce thickens and can coat the back of a spoon.

Béarnaise Sauce: In a double boiler, mix the yolks and lemon juice, and whip until it starts to thicken. Add melted butter slowly. Add salt and cayenne pepper to taste. Add tarragon; stir.

4 8-oz. double-lobe chicken breasts
Salt and pepper to taste
4 1-oz. slices of ham
Rochambeau Sauce
Béarnaise Sauce

1 small onion, chopped
4 tbsp. butter
4 tbsp. flour
3 tbsp. sugar
¼ cup white vinegar
10 oz. brown chicken stock
Salt and white pepper to taste

8 egg yolks
2 tbsp. lemon juice
1 cup warm, melted butter
Salt and cayenne pepper to taste
2 tbsp. tarragon

Eggnog Bread Pudding with Praline Rum Sauce

Preheat oven to 350 degrees.

Combine all ingredients in a baking dish; bake for 35 to 45 minutes until firm.

Cut into 4 portions. Top with praline rum sauce, whipped cream, and a mint leaf. **Serves 4**

Praline Rum Sauce: Mix melted butter and confectioners' sugar; cook until it thickens and lightly browns, then add rum.

4 cups stale, cubed French bread
6 large eggs, beaten
3 oz. golden raisins
Pinch of salt
4 tbsp. granulated brown sugar
2 tbsp. vanilla
1¼ cups eggnog
Praline Rum Sauce
Whipped cream, for serving
4 mint leaves, for serving

½ cup melted butter
¾ cup confectioners' sugar
3 oz. dark rum

175

ARNAUD'S
RESTAURANT

Holiday Eats

Founded in 1918 by Count

Arnaud Cazenave, Arnaud's is a venerable institution in the annals of New Orleans fine dining. Located at 813 Bienville Street in the French Quarter, the one thousand-seat restaurant is dramatically decorated for the holiday season, especially in the main dining room, where huge wreaths hang on the large beveled, glass windows, and handsome, old crystal chandeliers sparkle.

Réveillon dinners during the holiday season offer a nightly treat of specialties such as Crawfish Cakes with Creole Mustard Cream Sauce and Wilted Bok Choy. Even the Creole Onion soup is a special treat, served with a puff pastry topping, and the Pan Seared Duck Breast with Jalapeño-Orange Cane Glaze and Cassoulet Beans offers gourmet dining at its best. While the three-course meal by executive chef Tommy DiGiovanni is sure to delight, what could end a meal more delightfully than your very own Bûche de Noël? The fine Christmas log emphasizes its decidedly French origins behind the elegant Creole cuisine.

Arnaud's is open nightly, and the Jazz Bistro that overlooks Bourbon Street is available on request. There, you will hear live Dixieland Jazz that will make your meal truly a memorable event.

Nothing captures the joyous holiday dining spirit more than Arnaud's. You will be treated royally and enjoy some of the finest food in New Orleans.

OPPOSITE: **Arnaud's is aglow at Christmastime. Café Brûlot brightens any menu.**

TOP: **A grand réveillon dinner is featured at Arnaud's.**

LEFT: **Bûche de Noël.**

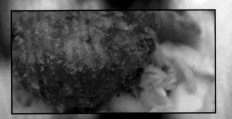

1 cup peeled shrimp, $^{90}/_{100}$
1 egg white
1 tbsp. minced shallots
1 tsp. red chili flakes
1 tbsp. fresh dill
⅛ cup heavy cream
Kosher salt to taste
1 cup minced crawfish tails
¼ cup breadcrumbs
2 cups Panko breadcrumbs
1 cup vegetable oil

½ tbsp. minced shallots
½ cup white wine
½ cup heavy cream
2 tbsp. Creole mustard
Kosher salt to taste

2 tbsp. olive oil
1 shallot, minced
½ head bok choy, julienned
Kosher salt to taste

2 tbsp. olive oil
1 large yellow onion, peeled and julienned
1 clove garlic, minced
1 sprig fresh thyme
½ cup dry sherry
1 tsp. Worcestershire sauce
½ bay leaf
1½ qt. veal stock
¼ cup blond roux
1 cup heavy cream
Salt and black pepper to taste
2 tbsp. chopped parsley
1 12" x 16"-sheet puff pastry dough
1 egg, beaten

Crawfish Cakes with Creole Mustard Sauce

Filling: Pat the shrimp dry, and place in a food processor. Purée the shrimp for 1 minute, and add the egg white. Purée until smooth; add shallots, red chili flakes, and dill, and purée for 1 minute more. Scrape down the sides of the processor bowl, then add heavy cream and salt. Transfer to a stainless steel bowl, and add minced crawfish tails and breadcrumbs. Fold together with a rubber spatula. Refrigerate, covered, overnight.

Divide the crawfish cake mixture into 4 four parts, or 8 parts if making mini crawfish cakes. Form into cakes, and coat with Panko breadcrumbs.

Preheat oven to 350 degrees.

Add vegetable oil to a 10" sauté pan over medium-high heat. Place cakes in the pan and pan-fry until golden brown, about 3 minutes on each side. Transfer to a baking pan and bake for 10 minutes until cooked through. Serve warm with Creole Mustard Cream Sauce and Wilted Bok Choy. **Yields 4 crawfish cakes or 8 mini cakes**

Creole Mustard Cream Sauce: In a small saucepan over low heat, add shallots and wine. Let simmer for 5 minutes. Add heavy cream and reduce by one quarter. Add Creole mustard and whisk to combine. Add salt to taste.

Wilted Bok Choy: In a large skillet over medium-high heat, add the oil. Add shallots, and sauté until translucent. Add the julienned bok choy; sauté until lightly wilted, about 2 minutes. Season with salt to taste. Keep warm until ready to use.

Creole Onion Soup en Croute

In a 4-quart stock pot, add oil and place over medium heat. Add onion, and sauté until caramelized, about 15 minutes, stirring so as not to burn onions. Add garlic and thyme, and sauté for 2 minutes. Deglaze the pan with sherry and Worcestershire sauce. Add bay leaf and stock. Reduce to medium heat. Let simmer for 10 minutes, then stir in roux. Add heavy cream, and whisk to remove any lumps. Simmer for 15 minutes, then add salt, pepper, and parsley.

Ladle into 4 bouillon cups, leaving ½" at the top of the cup.

Preheat oven to 375 degrees.

Place the puff pastry dough on a cutting board. Using a 4¾" round pastry cutter, cut out 4 circles. Using a pastry brush, brush the puff dough with the beaten egg. Place the dough, egg-side down, on top of the bouillon cups. Gently press the dough tops around the rim of the cups so the dough adheres to the cup. Using a pastry brush, brush the top of the puff pastry with the remaining egg. Bake for 15 to 18 minutes until tops are golden brown. Serve immediately. **Serves 4**

Pan-Seared Duck Breast with Jalapeño-Orange Cane Glaze and Cassoulet Beans

Coat the skin of the duck breast with blackening spice.

Place a sauté pan over medium heat, and add olive oil. When the pan is smoking hot, place the duck breasts skin-side down, and render the fat until golden brown, about 6 to 7 minutes.

Turn the duck breasts over, and sauté flesh side for 2 to 3 minutes; it should be medium-rare at this point. Remove from the pan and let rest for 3 to 5 minutes.

To assemble, slice the duck breasts as thinly as possible on a slight bias, and fan over cassoulet beans on a large dinner plate. Lightly drizzle the cane glaze over the duck breast. Garnish with the fresh thyme sprigs, and serve. **Serves 4**

Cassoulet Beans: Place a 1-gal. stock pot over medium heat, and add the diced bacon. Render bacon halfway. Add onions, garlic, and thyme, and sauté for 3 minutes until onion is translucent.

Add beans, chicken stock, and red chili flakes. Reduce heat, and let simmer, covered, for 45 minutes to 1 hour, depending on desired texture. Add salt if needed. Remove from heat until ready to serve.

Jalapeño-Orange Glaze: Add jalapeño, orange zest, garlic, and cane syrup to a 1-qt. stock pot. Turn to high heat and bring to a boil for 2 minutes. Add the glace, set heat to low, and reduce by half. Remove from heat until ready to use.

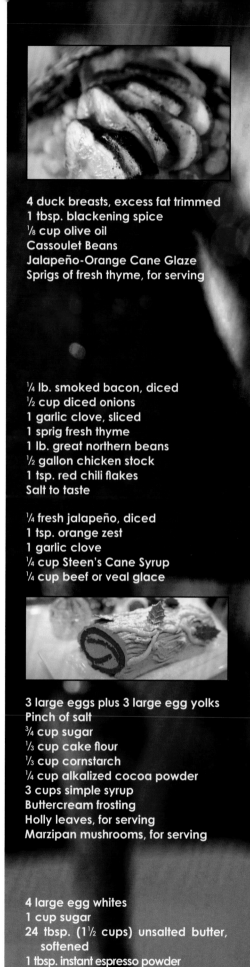

4 duck breasts, excess fat trimmed
1 tbsp. blackening spice
⅛ cup olive oil
Cassoulet Beans
Jalapeño-Orange Cane Glaze
Sprigs of fresh thyme, for serving

¼ lb. smoked bacon, diced
½ cup diced onions
1 garlic clove, sliced
1 sprig fresh thyme
1 lb. great northern beans
½ gallon chicken stock
1 tsp. red chili flakes
Salt to taste

¼ fresh jalapeño, diced
1 tsp. orange zest
1 garlic clove
¼ cup Steen's Cane Syrup
¼ cup beef or veal glace

Bûche de Noël

Preheat oven to 400 degrees. Grease a ½-size sheet pan.

Whisk the eggs, egg yolks, salt, and sugar in a saucepan over low heat (100 degrees) until thickened so it can coat the back of a spoon.

In a separate bowl, sift together cake flour, cornstarch, and alkalized cocoa powder. Fold dry ingredients into egg mixture. Spread batter into prepared pan.

Bake for 10 to 12 minutes.

Brush cake with simple syrup, then cover the top with buttercream frosting in an even, thin layer. Use parchment paper to help roll cake into a log, and chill. Cover log with remaining buttercream, and use a fork to make bark-like design on the log. Decorate with holly leaves and marzipan mushrooms. **Serves 12**

Buttercream Frosting: Whisk eggs and sugar in a saucepan over low heat until sugar is dissolved; remove from heat.

Using paddle attachment, beat butter into egg mixture 1 tbsp. at a time.

Dissolve instant espresso powder in the rum or brandy. Add mixture to buttercream; beat until combined.

3 large eggs plus 3 large egg yolks
Pinch of salt
¾ cup sugar
⅓ cup cake flour
⅓ cup cornstarch
¼ cup alkalized cocoa powder
3 cups simple syrup
Buttercream frosting
Holly leaves, for serving
Marzipan mushrooms, for serving

4 large egg whites
1 cup sugar
24 tbsp. (1½ cups) unsalted butter, softened
1 tbsp. instant espresso powder
2 tbsp. rum or brandy

NOLA
RESTAURANT

Holiday Eats

NOLA is one of Emeril Lagasse's three restaurants

in New Orleans, the other two being Emeril's and Emeril's Delmonico. All three reflect Chef Lagasse's high standards for providing interesting cuisine that always pays homage to the great Creole heritage of New Orleans. The headquarters for all of Chef Emeril's operations is located at his company's headquarters on historic St. Charles Avenue in the city.

OPPOSITE: NOLA's réveillon dinner features interesting choices.

BELOW: Pork cheek boudin-stuffed quail with Abita-braised collard greens and Steen's drizzle.

NOLA is the only Lagasse-driven restaurant in the French Quarter. Located at 534 St. Louis Street in a historic building just a block away from the Mississippi River, it presents a unique réveillon dinner menu featuring classic favorites such as Oysters Rockefeller—but not the usual baked version, rather, a soup laced with Herbsaint cream—and a main dish of Pork Cheek Boudin-Stuffed Quail with Abita-Braised Collard Greens and Steen's Drizzle.

For non-Louisiana residents, some of those ingredients won't mean very much. But for locals, the words alone invoke the glory of Emeril's modern Creole cooking imbued with local pride. The collards are braised in our very own Abita Amber beer, and the Steen's Cane Syrup from North Louisiana gives a touch of sweetness. When Abita beer isn't being used to flavor collard greens, it is usually consumed at local bars or one of the countless festivals in New Orleans and around the state, while Steen's Cane Syrup is used to glaze hams, coat popcorn balls, flavor pecan pie, and pour on biscuits or pancakes. Only NOLA's chef de cuisine, Josh Laskay, and Emeril himself would come up with such interesting dishes.

To end the meal, NOLA's pastry chef, Amy Lemon, offers a dessert, Pecan Pie Bread Pudding with Bourbon Anglaise, Sweet Potato Ice Cream, and Caramel Sauce. Imaginative? Yes. Delicious? Definitely. It has lots of local flavors perfect for your next holiday party. This is truly good eating.

Pork Cheek Boudin-Stuffed Quail with Abita-Braised Collard Greens and Steen's Drizzle

12 quail, cleaned, rinsed, and patted dry
Salt and freshly ground black pepper to taste
Pork cheek boudin, for stuffing
Olive oil, for brushing
Creole seasoning to taste
Abita-braised collard greens, for serving
Steen's cane syrup, for drizzling

Preheat oven to 400 degrees, and line a large baking sheet with aluminum foil.

Season the quail, inside and out, with salt and pepper. Using a spoon and your fingers, carefully stuff the cavity of each quail with as much stuffing as will fit, usually about 3 tablespoons per quail. Truss each quail with kitchen twine so that its legs are crossed and brought in close to the breast. (It should look like the birds are trying to cross their legs.) Arrange the stuffed quail on the baking sheet and brush or rub each bird lightly with olive oil to coat. Sprinkle lightly with Creole seasoning.

Roast the birds in the oven until just cooked through and the juices run clear, 15 to 18 minutes.

Remove the birds from the oven and remove the trussing. Place some of the collard greens and some of the pot liquor in wide, shallow bowls, and place the quail on top of the greens. Drizzle lightly with cane syrup, and serve immediately. **Serves 6**

2 oz. Applewood-smoked bacon, chopped
1½ lbs. pork cheeks, trimmed of silver skin and any tough membranes, cubed
1 onion, chopped (2 cups)
½ cup chopped celery
½ cup chopped bell pepper
2 tbsp. minced garlic
Kosher salt and freshly ground black pepper to taste
Cayenne pepper to taste
1 bay leaf
2 cups chicken stock or broth
½ lb. duck livers
1 tbsp. bourbon
1 cup long-grain white rice, cooked according to package directions (about 3½ cups cooked rice)
1 bunch green onions, thinly sliced

Pork Cheek Boudin: In a heavy-bottomed pan or small Dutch oven, render the bacon over medium heat until crisp. Add the pork cheeks, onion, celery, bell pepper, and garlic, and season lightly with salt, black pepper, and cayenne. Add the bay leaf and cook until the vegetables are soft and translucent, 6 to 8 minutes. Add the chicken stock and bring to a boil. Reduce heat to a simmer, partially cover, and cook for 1 hour to 1 hour and 15 minutes, or until the meat is very tender. Add the duck livers and the bourbon, and continue to cook, partially covered, for 30 minutes longer. Remove from heat, and allow to cool briefly. Remove the bay leaf, and add enough salt, pepper, and cayenne so that the cooking liquid is well-seasoned.

Working in batches, purée the mixture with the cooking liquid in a food processor until smooth. Transfer to a mixing bowl, and fold in the cooked rice and green onions. Season to taste with salt, pepper, and cayenne, and set aside until ready to stuff the quail. This may be made up to several days in advance and refrigerated in an airtight container. Any extra stuffing may be frozen for future use or heated and served alongside the stuffed quail. **Makes enough stuffing for at least 24 quail**

Abita-Braised Collard Greens: Render the bacon in a large saucepan over medium-high heat until crisp. Add the onion and cook until soft and translucent, 6 to 8 minutes. Add the garlic and cook until fragrant, 1 to 2 minutes. Add the chicken stock, beer, brown sugar, and vinegar, and bring to a gentle simmer. Add the greens in batches, waiting until the greens wilt into the cooking liquid before adding more. Season with salt, pepper, and cayenne, and cook over medium heat until the greens are tender, about 1 hour or longer. Taste and adjust the seasoning, and serve the greens in shallow bowls with some of the pot liquor. **Serves 6 to 8**

Recipe by Chef Josh Laskay, courtesy Emeril Lagasse and NOLA Restaurant

5 oz. Applewood-smoked bacon, chopped
2 medium onions, julienned
¼ cup minced garlic
1 qt. chicken stock or broth
1 12-oz. Abita Amber beer
¼ cup light or dark brown sugar
¼ cup apple cider vinegar
3 bunches (2½ lbs.) collard greens, stems removed, torn into pieces
Salt and freshly ground black pepper to taste
Cayenne pepper to taste

Oyster Rockefeller Soup with Herbsaint Cream

To make the Herbsaint Cream, place ½ cup Herbsaint in a small sauté pan over medium-high heat, and bring to a boil. Carefully tip the pan to ignite the liquor, and cook until the flame subsides and the liquor is cooked off, leaving about 3 tablespoons remaining in the pan. Set aside to cool. In a small bowl, blend the sour cream with the buttermilk, and then stir in as much of the flamed Herbsaint as necessary to make a smooth cream for drizzling. Season with salt and pepper to taste. Set aside until serving the soup.

To make the soup, place the oysters in a sieve and measure the oyster liquor. If liquid makes 1½ cups, proceed with the recipe. If not, measure the existing liquor and then add enough extra water to make 1½ cups; place oysters in a bowl along with the liquor and water and allow to sit for 1 hour. This will flavor the water and increase the liquor to the amount necessary to make the soup.

In a heavy saucepan, render the bacon with the garlic over medium heat. Once most of the fat has rendered, add the onion, celery, and bell pepper, and cook until the vegetables are tender and translucent. Add the oyster water, oysters, and heavy cream, and bring to a boil. Add the spinach, remaining 3 tbsp. Herbsaint, and salt and pepper to taste. Remove from the heat and allow to cool briefly. Working in small batches, purée the soup in a blender until completely smooth. Once all of the soup has been puréed, return the soup to the saucepan and keep warm until ready to serve. Taste and adjust seasoning if necessary.

To serve, ladle the soup into shallow soup bowls and serve drizzled with the Herbsaint Cream. **Serves 6 to 8**

Note: For an extra-special presentation, serve the soup garnished with a crispy fried oyster. You will need to purchase 6 to 8 additional oysters.

Recipe by Chef Josh Laskay, courtesy Emeril Lagasse and NOLA Restaurant

½ cup plus 3 tbsp. Herbsaint, divided
½ cup sour cream
1 tbsp. buttermilk
Salt and freshly ground black pepper to taste
1 pt. shucked raw oysters, with their liquor
5 oz. Applewood-smoked bacon
3 tbsp. minced garlic
2 cups chopped onion
½ cup chopped celery
½ cup chopped bell pepper
1¾ cups heavy cream
10 oz. baby spinach

Frisée Salad with Smoked Salmon, Toasted Almonds, and Tarragon-Citrus Vinaigrette

1 6-8-oz. salmon fillet
Salt and freshly ground black pepper to taste
Zest and juice of 1 lemon
Zest and juice of 1 lime
Zest and juice of 1 orange
½ bunch parsley, chopped
½ cup chopped tarragon leaves
2 cloves garlic, minced
1 shallot, minced
1 tsp. Dijon mustard
1½ cups vegetable or grapeseed oil
½ cup olive oil
1 large or 2 small heads frisee lettuce, torn into bite size pieces (6 to 8 cups loosely packed)
½ cup sliced toasted almonds, for garnish

Prepare a home smoker according to manufacturer's instructions, and preheat to 225 degrees.

Season the salmon on all sides with salt and pepper and transfer to the smoker; smoke until medium-rare, 8 to 12 minutes. Remove the salmon from the smoker, and set aside until cool.

Make the vinaigrette by combining all of the citrus juice and zest, parsley, tarragon, garlic, shallots, and mustard in a blender. While the blender is running, add the oils in a slow but steady stream until completely incorporated. Season to taste with salt and pepper.

Place the frisée in a salad bowl and add enough of the vinaigrette to coat the lettuce. Toss gently but thoroughly, and then transfer the lettuce to 6 to 8 salad plates. Using your fingers, gently flake the salmon into thin flakes and divide evenly among the plates on top of the lettuce. Drizzle a bit more vinaigrette over the salad and around the edge of the plate. Garnish with almonds, and serve immediately. **Serves 6 to 8**

Recipe by Chef Josh Laskay, courtesy Emeril Lagasse and NOLA Restaurant

Pecan Pie Bread Pudding with Bourbon Anglaise, Sweet Potato Ice Cream, and Caramel Sauce

2 cups heavy cream
2 cups milk
⅔ cup granulated sugar
2 tsp. ground cinnamon
1 vanilla bean, halved and seeds scraped
8 eggs
⅔ cup light brown sugar
1 lb. day-old brioche or challah bread, cut into 1" cubes
1 tbsp. butter
8 oz. toasted pecan pieces
Pecan pie filling
Sweet potato ice cream, for serving
Bourbon anglaise, for serving
Caramel sauce, for serving

In a medium saucepan, combine the heavy cream, milk, granulated sugar, cinnamon, and vanilla bean, and bring just to a boil. Set aside, and let the vanilla infuse in the cream mixture for 20 minutes.

Meanwhile, in a mixing bowl, whisk the eggs together with the brown sugar until thickened and well combined.

After the hot cream has infused for 20 minutes, return the cream mixture just to a boil; remove from heat. Little by little, whisk some of the hot cream mixture into the egg mixture, then whisk the egg mixture into the hot cream mixture in the saucepan.

Place the bread in a large, heatproof bowl. Strain the hot egg and cream mixture through a fine mesh sieve into the bowl with the bread, and allow the bread to soak, stirring gently every now and then, for 30 minutes to 1 hour.

Preheat the oven to 350 degrees. Butter a 5-quart deep baking dish, such as a lasagna pan, with the butter.

Transfer the bread mixture to the pan. Bake for 35 to 40 minutes, or until the pudding feels somewhat set to the touch but still slightly loose. Remove from the oven, and allow to sit for 10 minutes.

Sprinkle the top of the bread pudding with the toasted pecans, and then pour the pecan pie filling evenly over the top. Return the bread pudding to the oven, and cook until the pudding and topping are both set, 15 to 20 minutes. Remove from the oven and allow to cool briefly before serving.

To serve, cut or spoon a portion of the pudding onto serving plates, and garnish with a scoop of the sweet potato ice cream. Spoon the bourbon anglaise around the pudding, and drizzle with caramel sauce. **Serves 16 to 20**

Pecan Pie Filling: In a heatproof mixing bowl, whisk the eggs until frothy.

In a small saucepan, combine the light and dark corn syrups, brown sugar, and butter, and bring to a boil. Remove from the heat and whisk in the bourbon, vanilla, and salt. Pour this hot mixture into the eggs, and whisk thoroughly to combine. Set aside.

4 eggs
⅔ cup light corn syrup
⅔ cup dark corn syrup
⅔ cup light brown sugar
2⅔ tbsp. butter
⅓ cup bourbon
1½ tsp. vanilla extract
½ tsp. salt

Sweet Potato Ice Cream: Preheat oven to 400 degrees.

Place the sweet potato on a small baking sheet and bake until very tender, about 1 hour. Remove from the oven and set aside to cool.

Prepare an ice bath in a large bowl and set a slightly smaller bowl in the ice on top.

Once sweet potato is cool, peel and then pass the flesh through a sieve into a medium saucepan, discarding any strings or lumpy bits. Add the milk, cream, sugar, nutmeg, cinnamon, and cloves to the saucepan, whisk to combine, and bring to a boil.

Meanwhile, in a heatproof bowl, whisk the egg yolks until smooth.

When the sweet potato mixture is just at a boil, whisk about 1 cup of the hot sweet potato mixture, little by little, into the eggs, then whisk the egg mixture into the remaining sweet potato mixture in the saucepan. Cook, whisking constantly, until the mixture thickens enough to coat the back of a spoon. Working quickly, strain the sauce through a fine mesh sieve into the bowl sitting on top of the ice bath, and stir the mixture until it has cooled to room temperature. Transfer the mixture to the refrigerator until it is completely chilled, at least 2 hours or overnight.

Process the mixture in an ice cream machine according to manufacturer's instructions, and then transfer the ice cream to the freezer until ready to serve. **Makes about 1½ quarts**

1 sweet potato (about 1 pound)
2 cups milk
1 cup heavy cream
1 cup sugar
2 tsp. ground nutmeg
2 tsp. ground cinnamon
½ tsp. ground clove
½ cup egg yolks (about 6 yolks)

Bourbon Anglaise: Prepare an ice bath in a large bowl, and set a slightly smaller bowl in the ice on top.

In a medium saucepan, bring the heavy cream and sugar to a boil.

Whisk the egg yolks in a small, heatproof bowl. Little by little, whisk about 1 cup of the hot cream mixture into the eggs, then whisk the egg mixture into the remaining hot cream in the saucepan. Cook, whisking constantly, until the mixture thickens enough to coat the back of a spoon. Working quickly, strain the sauce through a fine mesh sieve into the bowl sitting on top of the ice bath, and stir the anglaise until it has cooled to room temperature. Stir in the bourbon and vanilla extract. Transfer sauce to the refrigerator until it is completely chilled, at least 2 hours or overnight. This can be made and refrigerated up to several days in advance. **Makes about 3 cups**

2 cups heavy cream
½ cup sugar
½ cup egg yolks (about 6 yolks)
¼ cup bourbon
1 tbsp. vanilla extract

Caramel Sauce: In a medium, heavy-bottomed saucepan, combine the sugar, water, and corn syrup. Bring to a boil over medium high heat, swirling the pan occasionally, until the sugar is completely dissolved. Continue to cook until the sugar begins to caramelize around the edge of the pan. Cook, swirling the pan occasionally, until the caramel is a deep amber color. Working carefully to avoid splatters, add the heavy cream and salt all at once and then return the pan to low heat. Cook, stirring occasionally, until the caramel has melted into the cream to form a smooth caramel sauce. Remove from heat, and allow the sauce to cool to room temperature.

Sauce may be served warm or at room temperature and may be made up to 1 week in advance and refrigerated until ready to use. Return to room temperature or microwave briefly before serving. **Makes about 1 quart**

All dessert recipes by Pastry Chef Amy Lemon, courtesy Emeril Lagasse and NOLA Restaurant

2½ cups sugar
1 cup water
½ cup light corn syrup
3 cups heavy cream
½ tsp. Kosher salt

WINDSOR COURT HOTEL

Holiday Eats

You don't have to go to London to enjoy teatime.

OPPOSITE: **The Christmas tree at the Windsor Court Hotel.**

BELOW: **Santa Claus at the Windsor Court.**

BOTTOM: **The grand tea in Le Salon of the Windsor Court Hotel is a lovely spread.**

Le Salon in the Windsor Court Hotel offers the grand experience of high tea in a comfortable setting just off the main lobby. Here you will find twenty-six choices of fine loose-leaf teas brewed in the grand manner; a menu of tea sandwiches, scones, and desserts; and even a harpist to make the experience complete.

Holiday tea in Le Salon is a memorable occasion in a backdrop decorated with a large Christmas tree loaded down with colorful ornaments and enough packages under the tree to keep any Christmas Grinch at bay.

It is in this joyful holiday setting that Angela Hill, an icon of nightly news in New Orleans on the CBS affiliate WWL and now with a popular weekday radio talk show, invited a few friends to join her for holiday tea: Laura Claverie, a well-known freelance writer; Meg Farris, a long-time reporter at WWL; and Clem Goldberger, associate vice president of marketing for the National World War II Museum. While the quartet, dressed in holiday finery, sipped tea and sampled tea sandwiches fit for a queen, the celebration event provided another way of celebrating the holidays in New Orleans.

"Tea at the Windsor Court is always a grand occasion," Angela says. "The holidays just make it a bit more special, with the festive mood greatly enhanced by all of the Christmas decorations."

Two selections of scones—regular and cranberry-orange—arrived, along with a variety of toppings. When it was time for the plates of desserts to appear, champagne was served and toast for the holiday season ended a perfect teatime.

ABOVE: **Desserts.**

LEFT: **Champagne.**

BELOW: **Sandwiches.**

OPPOSITE, LEFT: **Scones.**

OPPOSITE, RIGHT: **Toppings for scones.**

Cranberry-Orange Scones

Preheat oven to 450 degrees.

In a standing mixer fitted with a paddle attachment, or with an electric handheld mixer, combine the first five ingredients (through orange zest). Cut in butter until evenly combined and pieces are small (about the size of peas).

Add buttermilk to bind dough together. Fold in cranberries by hand. Then, gather the dough and turn out onto a lightly floured work surface.

Roll dough into a large rectangle. Fold the rectangle into thirds (like a business letter), and roll out until 1¾" thick.

Punch out scones with a circular or triangular cookie cutter, and let rest for 20 to 60 minutes in the refrigerator. Once chilled, brush scones with beaten egg.

Place scones on a baking sheet and place in the oven. Turn temperature down to 350 and bake for approximately 25 minutes until golden. Check at regular intervals to ensure even browning; rotate tray if necessary.
Serves 6

Recipe courtesy Shun Li, Windsor Court Hotel pastry chef

½ cup sugar
3 cups all-purpose flour, sifted
1 tbsp. plus 1½ tsp. baking powder
1½ tsp. salt
1 tsp. orange zest
1 cup cold butter, cut into cubes
2 cups buttermilk
½ cup dried cranberries
1 beaten egg, for brushing scones

ACKNOWLEDGMENTS

The first acknowledgement I must make is to thank the wonderful homeowners who welcomed me into their homes and so graciously allowed Cheryl to spend hours moving from room to room, capturing images of their holiday decorations. We are ever grateful for their kindness and consideration. We also owe a debt of gratitude to the staffs of each of the public historic homes featured in the book. Special appreciation goes to each person who aided us with scheduling the best times for Cheryl to photograph and each person who was prompt to furnish the material I needed to write the articles. The dedication of the Beauregard-Keyes, Gallier, and Hermann-Grima houses to remaining true to the decorating style of their respective periods and how the Longue Vue House and Gardens and the Williams Residence feature authentic holiday adornment create a legacy that makes visiting these locations during the Christmas season a truly remarkable experience.

By the time we had visited and photographed all seven beautiful Garden District mansions that were on the verge of opening for yet another Preservation Resource Center annual holiday tour, I was convinced it would be a bit of heaven to live in such grand homes. A special word of appreciation goes to all of the PRC staff who helped us with the scheduling and to the gracious homeowners who welcomed us into their homes amid the hustle and bustle of getting ready for thousands of people to tour their homes.

I have always known that some of the best dinners in New Orleans are served in private homes. I thought it would be an interesting addition to include some of the private holiday dinners in this book. Now, you can enjoy the gracious settings for meals and try the unique recipes each homeowner shared with us. A special thank you goes to Regina and Ron Keever, who included Mile High Pie on their menu; to Linda and Dr. Peter Tufton, who shared tasty family recipes for their holiday dinner; and to Kit and Billy Wohl, who love oysters so much, they included two oyster courses on their menu. You will marvel at the dessert table that takes over the dining room of Mary and Roland von Kurnatowski's St. Charles Avenue mansion when they have their annual holiday party. Mary personally prepares all of the goodies on the table, including the incredible Italian Cream Cake with Coconut Frosting, which she decorates with fresh roses. Her extra effort in preparing the recipes is so generous—in her mind, she just used a bag or box or bottle, but she took the time to retrace her steps. "Oh, Bonnie," she exclaimed. "I will have to run to the grocery store to tell you how many ounces for the bag and bottle—I just know which the right size is." Thank you, our special chefs, for your special contribution. Each of you did make a difference.

A special thank you to Antoine's executive chef Mike Regua, Arnaud's executive chef Tommy DiGiovanni, NOLA's chef Josh Laskay and pastry chef Amy Lemon, and the Windsor Court Hotel's pastry chef Shun Li. Cheryl and I also say a special thank you to Angela Hill, long-time star news anchor of

WWL-TV and now with her own WWL-radio show, for making our Tea at the Windsor Court Hotel story special by bringing three of her friends to enjoy the grand tea in the hotel's Grand Salon.

While this book features Cheryl Gerber's terrific photographs, we do need to thank photographer Jeff Strout and his company, Jeff Strout Photography, who stepped in to take the photographs of Mary and Roland von Kurnatowski's holiday party when Cheryl couldn't make it because of a long-time commitment for another assignment.

A special thank you to Peggy Scott Laborde, a talented friend I have always admired, for writing the foreword for this book. I never tire of watching Peggy's amazing collection of New Orleans documentaries that she has produced for WYES-TV. She is the co-author of *Christmas in New Orleans,* also a Pelican Publishing Company book, a true companion to this one.

Cheryl and I are ever grateful to Pelican Publishing Company for having faith in us to make a second book. Both of us are delighted with *New Orleans Historic Homes,* our first book, also published by Pelican. We were like wide-eyed children winning a spelling bee when the first book was finally released, and our first book signing felt a little like winning the lottery—we couldn't stop smiling.

Thank you to Kathleen Calhoun Nettleton, president of Pelican Publishing Company, and her staff, including talented Nina Kooij, editor in chief; Abi Pollokoff, my editor, who had the kindness of a favorite grandmother and patience of a saint; and all the staff for publishing our second book. Pelican Publishing is a venerable family-owned business, nationally recognized for excellence, with more than twenty-five hundred titles in print and a profusion of new titles offered each year. We are proud to be in such good company.

It is a great personal accomplishment to have written two books for Pelican, in addition to having had a more than a half-century career working first for a daily newspaper, then a weekly paper in Oak Ridge, Tennessee, before moving to New Orleans. My career writing for *New Orleans Magazine (NOM)* almost spans the entire life of the publication, and it was a great honor to serve as editor at one time. James "Jim" Autry, the editor of magazine, gave me my first assignment, and then decided I should write a monthly column, fashioned after the *New Yorker's* "Talk of the Town;" it's because of him that I launched the most exciting chapter of my career with *NOM.* When Jim became the editor of *Better Homes and Gardens* Special Interest Publications, I launched my career writing about architecture and interior design. "You must work for us," he said. It was in the late 1960s that I completed my first assignment for *Better Homes and Gardens Kitchen and Bath Ideas,* a piece about a group of interesting kitchens and bathrooms in New Orleans. Thank you, Jim, for being my mentor, and a special thanks to everybody with whom I have ever worked at *New Orleans Magazine.* I have been blessed, and my heart is full of appreciation.